THE QUOTE
HANDBOOK

ESSENTIAL STEPS TO BUILDING
THE PERFECT BOILER QUOTE

AARON MCLEISH

ISBN: 9798709592575

FIRST PUBLISHED JANUARY 2021 BY:
Aaron McLeish, Together We Build Limited

DESIGN BY:
Steven Baldwin, Noir

www.togetherwecount.co.uk

Dedication

To my amazing, beautiful daughter, Lola, you're my world and I love you unconditionally.

Table of Contents

Thank you

I would personally like to thank my business mentor, Mark Wickersham FCA. Mark kindly shared his vast knowledge of business and pricing and, due to this, I have gained extensive knowledge and helped many more clients at Together We Count (TWC). Without Mark's mentorship and support, *The Quote Handbook* would not have been possible so, I can't praise you enough for everything you do.

To all my loyal clients who, over the years, have put their trust in TWC to manage their financial affairs and listen to my advice. Thank you for your support and for being open to seeing business in a new light.

The following people also deserve a mention. Thank you for being invaluable in your own unique way:

Wayne Bettess – *Off the Tools Podcaster*

Erin Bradshaw-Priest

Carolina Cohen – *Lead Hero*

Lisa Crowther

Reza Hooda

Maira Jerome *(My Mum)*

Francis Rodino – *Lead Hero*

Sarah Stacey

Thank you everyone!

Foreword

The Off The Tools
Podcast
with Wayne Bettess

My name is Wayne Bettess and I'm the owner of YourNewBoiler.com and the founder of *Off the Tools* Podcast. For those who don't know me, I've been in the heating and boiler industry for more than 18 years, 10 of which were spent running my own business. Today, I also help small businesses across the sector to achieve greater success in life and business.

I won't lie, I've only recently got to know Aaron, but what a guy he is! Aaron's passion and love for this industry oozes out of him and he is far more than a standard Accountant! I recently had the pleasure of reading *The Quote Handbook* and was blown away by the depth of knowledge and expertise Aaron injected into this great book. Although I was already implementing some of the book's recommended strategies, I found *The Quote Handbook* to be immensely valuable because it covers the reasons and mind-sets behind these winning strategies. The knowledge and advice in the book is incredibly valuable whether you're just starting out on your own or you're already an established business owner.

Although Aaron is not a tradesperson, he has worked extensively in this industry and brings with him ideas and strategies that for most people will be new and exciting. More importantly, *The Quote Handbook* is packed with advice, tips, pointers and packages that you can implement pretty much straight away!

Well done for putting this book together and I look forward to reading your next one!

About the Author

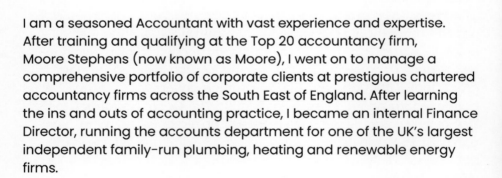

Aaron McLeish

TOGETHER WE COUNT

I am a seasoned Accountant with vast experience and expertise. After training and qualifying at the Top 20 accountancy firm, Moore Stephens (now known as Moore), I went on to manage a comprehensive portfolio of corporate clients at prestigious chartered accountancy firms across the South East of England. After learning the ins and outs of accounting practice, I became an internal Finance Director, running the accounts department for one of the UK's largest independent family-run plumbing, heating and renewable energy firms.

Today, I am the Managing Director of TWC, an accountancy firm which specialises in the plumbing and heating industry. Since starting the business in 2011, TWC has gone from strength to strength, providing accountancy services to businesses with a little something extra. And, with the wonders of modern technology, such as Xero, TWC now serves the entire country and international clients.
At TWC, I believe in educating my clients to be successful because your success will feel better if you're responsible for it. Along with all the services you expect from a traditional accountancy firm, I offer

a tailored business service, advising clients on how to achieve and maintain success. I share my current industry thoughts and present forward-thinking strategies to propel my client's business in the direction they choose. I also explain tax and accounting matters in a simple, understandable manner that leaves you empowered. No jargon, no complicated explanations, just straightforward, no nonsense, innovative advice for real genuine people like you.

I'm an expert accountant in the construction industry, in particular, the plumbing, heating and renewable sectors. My first-hand knowledge and experience of the struggles these businesses face alongside my ability to spot what makes one business stand out from the rest makes me different. I offer valuable advice from an accounting perspective to businesses of every size. I'm supported by a helpful, talented team of key individuals and work with trusted suppliers inside the trade.

Personally, I'm a family man and, when I'm not working, you'll find me at home, in the pub, or in my boxing gloves at the local sports club!

Who is *The Quote Handbook* for?

I have written *The Quote Handbook* for plumbing and heating installation engineers using an example of a combination boiler replacement. I've targeted this book at the plumbing and heating industries (and specifically at boiler installers), to give a working example and further explore how different sections of the perfect quote work in real-life scenarios.

The ideas, structures, concepts and elements contained within *The Quote Handbook* are transferrable to all trades undertaking domestic work. When quoting for commercial work, the quote needs to be more in-depth and will often have strict terms, such as payment applications and terms and conditions often dictated by the main contractor. This book, therefore, may not be relevant for commercial work.

If you follow the set structure within *The Quote Handbook*, it will also suit the following domestic service providers and tradespeople:

- Electricians
- Roofers
- Air conditioning and refrigeration installers
- Tilers
- General builders
- Carpenters
- Plasterers
- Carpet fitters
- Painters and decorators.

This list is not exhaustive.

Ultimately, it is my extensive knowledge and experience of the industry that led me to write *The Quote Handbook*. However, I want to make it extremely clear, I'm not a plumber or a gas engineer. I don't even know what gas looks like!

PART ONE

HOW TO BUILD THE PERFECT QUOTE AND BOOST YOUR BUSINESS

CHAPTER 1

Introduction

The Quote Handbook is an essential guide aimed at plumbing and heating-trade businesses who are struggling with the quotation process within their industry. Even if you're not struggling, this must-have book is for you!

You may not realise it, but there could well be room for improvements with your quotations. The reason many people struggle with quotations, estimates, prices and proposals is because no-one teaches it! School doesn't teach us how to write a quote, what needs to be included, how it should be structured for maximum results, or what the best practice is. Likewise, no-one tells you, "if you do it this way, you'll get x% more sales", or "if you do it this way, people are more likely to buy from you." There are no lessons, *until now...*

Ending the cycle of poor quotes

Most business owners either do what they think is right with no training, or they copy a quote from a competitor or previous employer thinking "that looks good, I'll copy that". Maybe, you just duplicate and paste the layout or the wording and use it with your company logo. The problem is, your competitors and previous employers were probably in the same boat as you and were not taught themselves. Hence, the cycle of poor quotes continues.

Tradespeople often do themselves an injustice. What information they do provide in the quote often misses out key elements which make up a perfect quote. In fact, what we're finding is that customers are missing out. They feel frustrated because they have asked for a quote, but the one given doesn't fulfil their needs. And, the business is missing out because they have not provided all the information the customer requires to make a decision. Changing this pattern could see the *company's quote conversion rate balloon significantly*. This translates to more money in their pocket along with happier customers and it becomes clear what the customer *is* or *is not receiving*. And, the company knows what has been agreed and what will be delivered, alleviating what is known as 'scope creep' (where more work is added to jobs prior to a price being agreed)!

I often find, when working with businesses, that the owner/director of the company are very good at going to customer's houses and saying "you need this kind of boiler because of X, Y and Z". But, the written side of the quote, which is what most customers need in order to process the information and help them make a decision, often falls short.

Perfecting the written quote

By writing *The Quote Handbook*, my intention is to take you through the sales process, from the initial enquiry to creating the perfect quote and presenting all the stages that matter in between. My emphasis remains on perfecting the written quote. Therefore, I will take you on a journey:

1. organising your first point of contact
2. visiting the customer at a property
3. making sure you're asking all the right questions
4. going away to write up the quote
5. issuing the quote, and
6. accepting the job.

Then, the rest is down to you to fulfil the job in hand.

I believe that a business has many 'shop windows', portraying its values, brand, style and ethos via visible channels, such as websites, vehicles, t-shirts and adverts. Producing a quote is another shop window which gives customers and potential clients a reflection of your business or the operation you run. Therefore, you should treat the entire quoting process with the consideration it deserves. The quote must not have any spelling or grammatical errors and should be presented in line with your brand guidelines. An impactful quote, if used in the right way, will impress a potential customer and encourage them to buy your products as well as positively demonstrate what you and your business are really about.

Mastering a quote template

Software companies charging a subscription to access bespoke quoting tools, in my eyes, don't enable the versatility which should be seen in quotes; therefore, Microsoft Word is a good starting ground for your quote template. But, I would suggest you produce a master quote template which is an in-depth template full of all of your standard wording, layout, ideas, products and services offered. This can then be cut down, edited and tailored to best meet a customer's bespoke requirements. You should view this template as a business system which needs to be constantly reviewed and continuously tweaked or improved.

Before we dive into the nitty-gritty and explain the steps to a winning quote, I will explain a few concepts and my thoughts on the subject. These set the scene and are important to include here. I feel sharing this information sets the foundations for both building and executing a perfect quote.

CHAPTER 2

I don't have time for this!

I often hear people say they don't dedicate enough time to making sure their quotes are perfect. It is already exactly how they like it; well written and ticks all the boxes. I would, however, like to open your eyes as to why, when quoting for a boiler installation it is so vital to get it right to ensure you win as many high-value jobs as possible.

What makes the most money?

A boiler installation involves one customer. A day 'on the tools' with no additional travel. All the materials are at hand after one trip to the supplier. Therefore, potentially, you could earn £500-£1,000 in labour alone just for one boiler installation. On the flip side, if you are a busy engineer with a lot of callouts for breakdowns, or plumbing and heating emergencies, then you may be able to do up to five jobs a day. But, that also means you have to answer five different calls, go to five separate houses, pick up parts for five different jobs, write up five job sheets, issue five invoices and all before chasing five customers for payment. Wouldn't it be worth putting a little extra time and effort into winning boiler installations?

Earn more, work less... surely that is the ideal work/life goal?

What I'm trying to say is *follow the money*. I don't want you to be a busy fool, but ensure you put in the time and effort for a decent boiler quote. If it is going to take you an extra hour out of your evening to make the quote perfect, then do it! If you win the quote, there's a great profit and reward in that, as opposed to being a busy fool, doing five routine services in a day or standard maintenance work. And, as you get used to quoting the way I'm going to suggest, the time to produce each one will reduce. Therefore, when I hear the comment "I don't have time" my response is "bloody well make time!"

I intend to save you time on the writing phase of producing a quote. I would suggest that you use the examples of the different sections in *The Quote Handbook* along with the wording (*A full example quote is at the end of the book, but I have copied the relevant section of it into each chapter, so you have an example as you go through the process*). Bulk them out even more to your choosing and general gut feeling. Include as much text, information, facts, figures, best practice into a quote template. Then, when a job comes in, simply delete non-relevant sections and cut it down to suit the customer's exact requirements.

As I mentioned before, put all your main effort into the first template, creating one you're really happy with and have this as the master file. But, using the *kaizen* concept (mentioned later), constantly add, tweak and improve this master template. Listen to your customers and, if repeat questions are being asked, then answer their problems within the template so that you have a documented response in the FAQs/other section. If you feel an area can be improved, do it, test it and take small steps to improve this master file. Times, people, trends, and technology change and you/your quoting system must adapt with them.

CHAPTER 3

Estimated business cost of producing a quote

As a business owner, have you ever added up the actual cost to your business for going out and quoting for a boiler replacement? Most companies offer free quotations, but adding up the cost can be eye-opening.

Such costs could comprise the following:

1. The initial telephone enquiry – it might be someone from your administration team, head office or answering service. Estimated cost **£10** (administration).

2. The surveyor drives to the property from the office. This may take half an hour. Estimated cost **£25** (fuel and time).

3. The surveyor spends time at the property to assess the work taking another hour or more of their time. Estimated cost **£50** (time).

4. The surveyor travels from the property back to the office, incurring more fuel and time costs. Estimated cost **£25** (fuel and time).

5. Back in the office, the surveyor adds up the cost of materials, works out how much labour they would need (the day-rate) then puts the quote together and sends the quote via email or

post. Hopefully, there is also a follow up procedure for the quote, which adds further administration time. This element of the quote could take a couple of hours. Estimated cost **£50** (time and administration).

Straight away, you have a conservative and estimated base cost for one boiler survey and quote of **£160** – bearing in mind this is not the total cost to the business.

This is without factoring in the advertising costs or the cost of getting the lead. You have not factored in the lost opportunity cost, i.e. if that surveyor was a tradesperson and also does callouts, what opportunities have they missed out on to provide a quote that goes nowhere? They could have earned £80 per hour + VAT for attending a breakdown callout, or for fixing a leak. The figures soon stack up. If you're going out to quote 10 jobs per week but only win five of them, then you have a conversion rate of 50%. That is costing the company over £800 per week (5 x £160). Look at that over a month or a year (52 x £800 = £41,600), or even worse, over the lifetime of a business. The figures can get pretty hefty! This is called a 'sunk cost' in accounting. How are you as a business recovering this sunk cost?

My point is – it's so important to get the quoting process right because the cost to a business of not quoting successfully could mean make or break for your business. If you're quoting for jobs but never getting the work, then there's a problem with the process, the system and these need addressing. No business can survive extensive sunk costs... the liquidators will not be far away.

I hope this illustrates the importance of getting the quoting system right because it could be the difference between dinner on the table and not!

CHAPTER 4

How to use *The Quote Handbook*

The Quote Handbook is a comprehensive guide to help you excel at building boiler quotes and setting great pricing strategies. With sections covering all areas of running a business, I suggest reading my entire book from start to finish. Then, dip into the chapters you want to implement straight away perhaps tackling the easiest sections first.

I recommend implementing one or a few ideas at a time. It may be a giant leap to implement everything in one go. Therefore, pick a chapter from the book, read it, study it and then implement it. Use the wording from my 'Example' quotes that you'll find at the end of every section. Then, when you're confident with that particular area of the quote, move onto another. Please take action though; you can lead a horse to water and all that...

At the end of *The Quote Handbook*, there is a full example of a boiler replacement quote template. Each section in this full example quote can be found at the end of the chapter it relates to, so you can see the example as you read through the book. However, each section will make more sense, of course, when you read the full example quotation at the end of *The Quote Handbook*.

CHAPTER 5

The *kaizen* concept

What is *kaizen*?

Kaizen is a Japanese term meaning 'change for the better' or 'continuous improvement'. It is a concept referring to business activities that continuously improve all functions and involve all employees from the Chief Executive Officer (CEO) to the assembly-line workers.

How can I apply *kaizen* to my quotes?

If you constantly review your quotes, making tweaks and amendments, your entire operation will be more efficient. Take time to consider if you're asked the same questions by customers. If so, perhaps the quote isn't clear enough and you could amend something on your template to answer that question in the future. Answering a common question could save valuable time in the quoting process.

There is no end to how you can apply *kaizen* to your business. A process successful at one time may not be as successful a year later. If you stay the same, but everything around you changes, then what you're doing will quickly become irrelevant. As more efficient ways of doing your job arises, you must adapt too. Small incremental changes to improve a business process will drive you forward, towards greater success.

CHAPTER 6

The initial enquiry

When a customer enquires about a new boiler replacement, this is the starting point to the boiler quotation. When a customer calls your business to tell you they need your services, it's at this point you need to establish if your business is right for the job or not. It's vital to pre-qualify the enquiry to make sure it's work you want.

If you go to a job only to discover that you can't do it (maybe it's a boiler that runs on oil and you don't have the qualification to do that), then you have wasted your time and theirs. In actual fact, the initial enquiry is particularly important for both parties.

It's a good idea to have an initial enquiry document with set questions to ask everyone and prompts to remind you of the areas you need to check out. That way, you will always ask all the right questions, and you can go to the job to scope out the premises with confidence that you can help. Below is an example of a standard customer new boiler enquiry form, with notes.

Customer's Name	
Telephone number *If possible, request an alternative number as well.*	
Email *Ask if you can add them to your mailing list – for marketing purposes.*	

Property address *Is the property in an area you serve? Explain to the customer you need to visit the location to provide a quotation. You want to see what is involved.* *There's a saying, "prescription without diagnosis is malpractice". So basically, to provide the remedy, you need to see what the problem is first. The only way to do this is to visit the property. Or, work off-plan, if it is a new build, etc.*	
Fuel type? Gas/oil/liquefied petroleum gas (LPG), etc. *If you don't offer services for all types of fuel, then you may wish to make a referral to a company that does. I would also suggest that you have a referral system in place. If you're passing oil leads to a different company, then make sure that you're getting some sort of commission for that or a referral back.* *Alternatively, suppose you're getting lots of enquiries into a certain technology or fuel type that you don't offer. You may want to consider getting certified in that area so you aren't passing leads on all the time, then the sale remains within your business. Don't leave money on the table!*	
Level of urgency *If your prospective client's boiler is down and they have no heating or hot water, aim to visit and quote on the same day. The customer will see that you care. Establish the urgency and act on it.*	
Time slot *People hate a morning or afternoon slot! Most people don't have time to give up half a day waiting for you to arrive. Give a two-hour window, or less if achievable.*	

Being polite and professional pays off

Along the entire customer journey, it's essential you remain professional, warm and courteous. The very first stage of a boiler quotation is the customer's initial enquiry, so when a potential customer rings you up, make sure you respond in a polite and professional manner. For example, "good morning, Superb Plumbing and Heating, this is Rachel speaking. How may I help you?" Doesn't this sound better than, "hello, who's this?" with loud noises in the background.

If you answer the phone with the latter example, then your potential customer will have the impression that you're unprofessional before you even begin. In contrast, the first example gives the right impression from the offset. Setting the tone on an initial telephone enquiry is crucial for the rest of the job. Don't mess up that first call!

If you find it difficult to answer calls when you're working, and don't have an office-based member of the team to do this for you, why not consider outsourcing to a telephone answering company? That way, your company will never miss a potential client and you're guaranteed a professional approach. The answering company can use your initial enquiry form to make sure all your details are correct. You then choose how and when to receive the enquiry. The completed enquiry form can be emailed to you (so you have a written record), or the information can be inputted straight into your database/CRM if you have one. The company answering your calls can even organise your diary, so they know when you are available to quote.

Outsourcing your calls and diary can both enhance your efficiency and present your company in an extremely professional light. And, the caller will never know that the person they were speaking to was not in your office.

CHAPTER 7

The home survey

When you arrive at a customer's house to identify what work is required, I recommend you're smartly dressed. Shoes, trousers, skirts and a shirt are preferable; a shirt with your logo is ideal. Big money is at stake so your appearance *must* be of a professional standard.

I advise not turning up in a grubby, dented work van with filthy overalls having just unblocked a toilet. Always turn up in clean, sign-written vehicles. If you show up in a dirty work van, that's got 'clean me' or 'I wish my wife was this dirty' written on the back in mud, it doesn't give a good impression about your business and your care and attention to detail. If you know you will be messy in the afternoon, book your quotes in the morning. And don't give the impression you have nipped in on your way home or on route to the pub.
If you're running late, let the customer know. Remember, you're entering their home, their castle – most probably their most valuable asset. Respect this fact.

Throughout *The Quote Handbook*, I'll be dropping little snippets of advice, ideas and clues to make you stand out from the crowd. In reality, when you do present your quote and it's more expensive than *Gavin the Gasman* down the road, the customer won't be taken aback because of the way you represented your company.

CHAPTER 8

Scoping out the work

Scoping out the work is probably the most crucial section of the quoting process; it is where you establish what's wrong, what the customer needs and why they need it. The only way to do this effectively is to ask questions – lots of questions and to investigate!

I'm going to break it down into elements, each aspect is vital to the next stage of the quote. What the customer tells you and what you establish will make up the body of the initial quote. Make sure you note down what the customer says, your findings and initial thoughts. Write down their exact words, as these can be regurgitated in the quote, showing you have listened, taken note and are on the same wavelength.

Building the pain

Don't be shy to ask lots of questions. The more you ask, the quicker you will work out what they want and need, and it also establishes you as a genuinely interested expert. You're the specialist and the customer will not know the answers. This is where your skills and expertise come into play. Your specialist knowledge means you will know what boiler would be ideal in their home.

Measure up! Don't forget to measure up and note how many radiators run off the appliance. That way, you know what capacity boiler is required for the specific household needs. You also need to establish what the customer's plans are for their property. Are they going to extend? Are they planning on converting the loft? Also, don't forget to ask how many people live in the property and how much hot water is used. All these answers dictate the current and future demands of the boiler and what capacity it needs to fulfil.

> *"Mr and Mrs Tyson, are you planning any house renovations in the next few years? Are you hoping to extend? Do you require 24-hour heating? How many people currently live here?"*

Establish the customer's pain points

Establish the customer's gripes. How long has the boiler been down? One day? A week? How is that inconvenient? The more 'pain points' you can get from the customer, the better, as you can use these to help you word your quote.

> *"Mr Calzaghe, you said your boiler's down. Have you had to go elsewhere for a shower? Have you had to wake up earlier than usual?"*

It's also at this time you would establish any additional works which the customer requires. How is the heating being controlled? Is it by Hive or a Nest system? Does the customer embrace technology? Do they want an app on their phone where they can heat their home an hour before they get there so it's nice and cosy on arrival?

With all the different technologies out there, you need to let your customer know about them. If you don't tell them, they will not know what's available. Always assume they don't know!

It's easy to stick to the standard questions when quoting for a replacement boiler. So, dive in and drill deep into people's real household issues. Demand to establish what a customer wants – it's the only way to come up with a solution.

The wish question

Ask the customer, *'if I could grant you a wish to solve anything heating and plumbing related, what would you choose?'* If you or your business can fulfil this wish then, guess what, it can be included in their quote!

CHAPTER 9

The fact-find

Questions, questions, questions...

Remember, the more questions you ask, the more comprehensive your quote will be.

Why do they need a new boiler? (Getting to know your customers)

Has it broken down, or is there another reason? People don't think or care about their boiler until it breaks down. New owners of a property will generally stick with the boiler which was installed when they purchased the house, only thinking about it when it stops working.

What effect does not having a working boiler have on a household?

Are there children in the house? This could make it more urgent for the homeowner.

Have they been putting off replacing it for a while? Most people would rather have a holiday than replace their boiler. They're happy to use their electric shower and boil the kettle whilst the weather's warm. Roll on the winter months and suddenly it's more important as they have no heating.

About the property

How many bathrooms do they have? If they have more than one, are they used at the same time by different people?

Do they have a separate shower and bath, or is the shower over the bath?

Are they planning to get any extensions on the property? If they're planning to build another bathroom, then their existing boiler may be inadequate for their needs, which will require additional expense and work.

Points to consider: Test the speed of the water to see what litres per minute they're getting. Some people think if they get a 40kw boiler, they're going to get the litres per minute it states in the boiler manufacturer's guidebook, but if you've got a 1,080 tap then a £2,000 boiler will not change that! Obviously, you don't need me to tell you this information – you're the specialist, after all, but explain your thought process to the customer. They won't think you're trying to pull a fast one if they understand why you're making the recommendations. Communication is key.

Is the boiler's warranty important to them?

Are they going to be in the house for a long time? If so, they probably want a new boiler with a longer manufacturer's warranty.

What's the reason they're changing the boiler?

If someone's boiler has broken down, they may not have a good credit rating for a finance option and they want a cheap boiler that works.

At the other end, there are customers who want the most energy-efficient boiler and plan on spending 10-20 years in the property. They may decide to bite the bullet now and get a top of the range boiler fitted. Therefore, reaping the energy efficiency reward over many years to come.

Are they interested in a 'smart' heating control system?

Pushing a smart heating control system like Hive onto a customer who is not tech savvy is pointless and not in the best interests of the customer. Trying to sell it to someone with a Motorola flip-phone is a waste of everyone's time. The customer really needs to have an iPhone or a decent Android, and the know-how to work it, for it to be beneficial. This is another example of how your knowledge and expertise can make the quote personal. Putting your customer's needs above the desire to make money will help to establish you as a trusted tradesperson.

CHAPTER 10

Your availability

Having an online diary or booking system could help you win quotes. You can look at the diary with the customer and discuss your availability there and then. Having access to the diary, or your logbook, wherever you are, means you can prioritise your bookings.

For example, if you have work to do on an empty house but a single parent with three kids has a broken-down boiler, you might postpone the empty house by a day or two and get the family home sorted as soon as possible. Showing a potential customer your availability and willingness to make changes for them will make you stand out if they're getting multiple quotes.

You could also offer a Fast Track service, explained later on in *The Quote Handbook* (*see* page 90).

CHAPTER 11

Testimonials

Showing a potential customer some of your testimonials is a great tool to gain the Know, Like and Trust factor.

What is the Know, Like and Trust factor?

Basically, it represents the journey that a person takes when getting to know your brand, business, or you. First, they have to KNOW you. Once they know you, they start to LIKE you and your brand or business. Once they know and like you, TRUST develops. Your customers must trust your service, your business and your ability to do the job and have confidence in what you plan to do.

Gaining great reviews

Great testimonials show potential customers that previous customers have used and rated your company. You've done the work, done an excellent job and made a good impression, so much so that they want to shout it from the rooftops (social media platforms, Yell.com, Checkatrade, Google reviews, etc!). Good reviews tell other people you are credible. Later in *The Quote Handbook*, I share some tips to systematically obtain testimonials, which then creates an upwards spiral of future customers to your business.

When you go to a customer's house, have some pre-printed testimonials which you can leave, along with your boiler brochure. (Steps for producing a boiler brochure are explained later in the book). Your potential customers can read your businesses literature, while considering their options as you measure up for their boiler replacement.

CHAPTER 12

Anchor

In business, it's vital to use an anchor when pricing. An anchor pricing strategy is when you use a price to give your customers a frame of reference for valuing your products and services.

An anchor can be used to make a price seem smaller. It draws attention to a *bigger* number so when you present your price, it looks *smaller*. This is known as a 'pricing psychology strategy'.

For example, in your boiler quotation you could state the average house price value in the UK is around £318,000 (December 2020, Zoopla.co.uk) and by installing a brand new, efficient combination boiler, this can add 4% to a property's value (yourepair.co.uk). Therefore, by adding a new boiler, you could add £12,720 to the value of the customer's property. The £12,720 (and even the £318,000) acts as an anchor making the boiler quote seem smaller than it is.

If you're putting together a quote for £3,000 and you mention it could add £12,720 in value to the property, it makes the price of the boiler at £3,000 a fantastic deal. In this example, the transaction is seen as pure profit. More value is added to the property after the cost of installing the boiler. The customer would gain a profit of £9,720 (£12,720 less £3,000)! This could make the buying decision a lot simpler for the customer having clearly established the gain to be made.

The power of the pricing psychology strategy

This powerful pricing psychology strategy could be the deciding factor for a customer to choose your business for a new replacement boiler because you have provided valuable information which your competitors wouldn't even have thought of! Your business will stand out.

I would suggest an anchor is used in the quote. Further on, I explain another anchor technique.

CHAPTER 13

The three stages of the quoting process

I have broken down the three stages of the quoting process into easy-to-follow steps, as follows:

Step One: Establish the problem.

Step Two: Build the problem.

Step Three: Capture the problem and rectify it.

Let's briefly consider each step in turn...

Establish the problem

The first stage of the boiler quotation is to fact-find and establish the problem. As you have already seen in the chapters above, fact-finding is about uncovering the facts, gathering information and identifying the customer's needs. This is the most crucial stage because there is a clear statistical link between the use of questions and a successful outcome in relationship selling.

Questions are so important, you should plan them carefully when preparing a boiler quote. Planning your questions is more important than planning what you will tell the customer. Don't rush the fact-find.

You SHOULDN'T start talking about your solution until you fully understand what is important to the customer, their home, their family, what they value and what they want.

You want to discover what their needs are, what they want from a heating system and about any future changes to their home and, therefore, heating requirements. This is the purpose of the fact-find. You need to know why you've been invited into someone's home to quote for a new boiler. Find out what has caused them to notice there is an issue with the boiler. Is the water pressure too low? Is the water not hot enough? Use your skills to dig deep here and find out what the client wants.

A lot of people don't know what they want! Your expertise can guide them through this by letting them know what the various solutions are. Could they benefit from improved technology? Are there some smart thermostatic radiator valves (TRVs) available which could save the customer money? Would they benefit from a smart home full of gadgets and gizmos, linked to their phone? Do they prefer the more traditional thermostat on the wall? Get to know your customer, their wants, needs and desires. Research shows the more questions you ask, the better your quote if you address the matters raised.

Always remember people love others being interested in them and being listened to, so, don't just note down their answers and move on. Repeat your understanding of what they've said back to them; this will give them confidence you've really 'heard' them and will do your best for them.

At the end of the visit, agree the date and time they'll receive the boiler quote and how it will be issued; via email (recommended), post or by hand. Ensure you establish when the customer would like their new boiler installed. If the boiler is condemned, this will be as soon as possible.

The next two sections are covered and included in the actual boiler quote.

Build the problem

Create your solution

When you execute the fact-find with diligence, you'll be in a better position to create a solution that specifically meets the customer's real needs (not necessarily what they asked for).

Now you're ready to present your quotation to the customer. I will explain in detail the different sections which must be included in a boiler replacement quote. The information, sections and wording used, all build up value. They inform the customer you are a skilled tradesperson who knows what they're doing and, as such, the customer will be delighted at the end of the installation. By fully explaining what you do, you're subtly planting a seed in the customer's head which builds value and, when the prices are revealed, it comes as less of a shock because they understand how much work goes into a boiler replacement.

In fairness, we've established why the client needs a new boiler but we now need to build on that. For example, the client said their boiler had broken down. This has resulted in them having to go to the gym for their morning shower, adding an hour to their morning routine, making them tired and more stressed, adding pressure on to the day. Extract as many pain points as possible. Don't see this process as a negative experience. You need to build on the problem, so you can then find a remedy. If you don't build it as much as possible, you're doing your client a disservice. They might tell you they need a new boiler, but you know it's going to be more. You need to understand and focus on these pain points to offer the best solution. If you don't, you won't be completing a thorough job. Ask enough questions so the customer can tell you what else a brand-new boiler and better heating controls will do to enhance their life.

Avoidance of pain:

Remember, "people are more motivated against the avoidance of pain than they are towards the motivation of gain." Diving into this saying and referring it to the context of *The Quote Handbook* would be as follows:

1. Fully-functional heating system.
2. Peace of mind knowing that the heating system is working.
3. Fewer worries and anxiety.
4. Safety regarding Co2 leaks.

Attainment of gain:

1. Cheaper heating bills.
2. Running hot water.
3. Heating.

Take advantage of the customer's pain points; the avoidance of pain is more powerful than the attainment of gain. This is why marketers often find pain-avoidance headlines achieve higher conversion rates.

Highlighting pain points

In this section, you can explain what the customer may be experiencing and also what they will experience if they don't act now – added continual stress.

For example, if a boiler has broken down, what's happening? The home-owner doesn't have any hot water and heating. They may be going to a friend's house for a shower or to the gym. You might want to explain to the customer their electricity costs have gone up because they have to use the emersion heater, which is much more expensive to use than a boiler. Their electricity bills are going to increase while their gas boiler isn't working. Highlight the negative impact the client is experiencing, the stress, the hassle – the pain!

All these examples are pain points. Further on in *The Quote Handbook*, there are some standard *pain points* for someone not having a working boiler in their home, these can be copied and pasted into your quote. Highlighting the pain points then showing your solution to alleviate the pain can be a potent conversion tool, so use it!

Capture the problem and rectify it

By now, you have questioned the customer, you have built the problem up and now you need to capture it. By capturing it, I mean offer a solution to their problem. In this instance, it's going to be a new boiler. You need to communicate to the client, how you're going to make their life better, what the result will be and clearly state why they need this solution in their life, to stop the pain (e.g. cold nights, inconvenience and less stress).

Turn the pain into benefits. For example, "don't worry, Mayweather Plumbing and Heating are here to save the day. We are fully trained tradespeople who have dedicated our lives to gas/oil/LPG/electrics to ensure your home is warm and cosy at all times".

The benefit is often the opposite of the pain. The advantage is your client will have running hot water and the central heating will soon be warming their home again. In reality, you've painted a picture of the pain and you've turned pain into a gain (what will be gained from repairing or replacing the boiler).

Create a quotation to confirm the price and scope of the boiler replacement work. A quote should detail exactly what you're going to do for the customer, as per the information obtained in the fact-find and state your solution.

If you haven't fully understood the customer's needs, wants and desires at the end of the fact-find meeting, then you will not be able to sufficiently inspire them to buy your solution as presented in your quote. You will be faced with objections and won't be able to capture the problem and rectify it. After you have presented the customer with their quote and they say something like, "I need to go away and think about it" it's usually their polite way of saying, "no, I don't want to go ahead with you or your company for this project". Sadly, you haven't managed to capture the problem and rectify it.

In your written quote, you should set out the problem, the consequences of their predicament, pain points and quantify these. You also want to explain the benefits of your proposed solution to the customer. Use pricing psychology to make your price seem small compared with the benefits. Set out your payment terms clearly. Reassure your customer with a guarantee where possible. Make it easy for your customer to say yes and proceed.

The table below demonstrates the different elements to a boiler quotation explored in *The Quote Handbook*. Where each section fits within the three stages of the boiler quotation is shown.

Please note: the 'Establish the problem' section is mainly the leg work undergone prior to the quote being written, therefore, this has already been covered when questioning and scoping out the job.

Three stages of the quotation:

- Establish the problem, scope out the work – ask questions, etc.
- Build the problem
- Capture the problem and rectify.

PART TWO

PRODUCING A PERFECT QUOTE – SECTION BY SECTION

Section of Quote	Content
1. The front page	**Establish the problem:** Customer's name and address, quote number, date, title.
2. Restate the pain/ problem	**Build the problem:** Restating the pain points of the problem to the customer.
3. Take the pain away	Detail how you will fix the problem, e.g. install new boiler with a thermostat, comply with building regulations, warranty, etc.
4. Your bespoke quote	The customer's tailored options and an exact outline of all work being undertaken.
5. Describe their options	Provide three options in a quote and offer greater choice to customers.
6. Set out everything you do	List everything you offer and add-ons. Explain to the customer more details on each feature can be found in the quote's appendix.
7. State your prices	Use pricing techniques.
8. Offer options	**Capture the problem and rectify it:** Extras, add-ons and optional extras. Offer behaviour rewards.
9. Warranties, guarantees and promises	Guarantee and warranty details – manufacturer's warranty and your company's guarantees/promises.
10. FAQs	Anything else relevant goes here.
11. T&Cs	Terms and conditions.
12. Call to action	Call to action.

CHAPTER 14

The front page

The first part of the quote is the front page; this needs to include the customer's name, address and a unique quotation number. It also needs to include a title for the quote, such as, 'Boiler Replacement – Upgrading Your Heating System'.

Use a title which engages the customer's feelings and emotions or, if possible, re-use your customer's own words in the title. You also need to have your company name and address along with your company registration number (if you're a limited company). You can also include your VAT number. Ensure your contact details are on there. Add the date the quotation has been produced, and, *never* forget your company logo.

It is also useful to state how long the quote is valid for. You don't want someone coming back to you in six months, after a considerable price rise in the cost of boilers or copper, insisting you honour your initial quote.

Personalise a customer's quote

To make the quotation even more unique to the customer, you could take a picture of their front door (or their door number) and insert the image on the front page to make it personal. It's a small gesture which shows you haven't just produced a generic quote which you send to everyone. It also demonstrates you have taken time and effort to put it together. Make it relevant to the customer; it is not about you; it is about them!

I also recommend using bold and eye-catching straplines, such as:

- Keeping you warm and cosy
- Creating heat and happiness
- Future-proofing the heat in your home
- Giving you that warm and cosy glow
- Bringing warmth and comfort back to your home.

SUPERB
PLUMBING & HEATING

123 New Street, Old Town, Newtoncity, NT8 4AB

www.superbplumbing.xx.xx   T: 0000 55378008   E: enquiries@superbplumbing.xx.xx

Boiler Replacement
Upgrading your Heating System

Keeping you warm and cosy.

QUOTATION NUMBER: Q12345

PREPARED FOR

Mr and Mrs Fury
34 Water Street, Smallville, S14 0TW

DATE: XX/XX/XXXX

This quotation is valid for 14 days.

REGISTERED OFFICE: SUPERB PLUMBING & HEATING LTD, 123 NEW STREET, OLD TOWN, NEWTONCITY, NT8 4AB

VAT NUMBER: XXXXXXXXXX CRN: XXXXXXXXXXXX

CHAPTER 15

Restate the pain/ problem

Section two of the quote is aimed at *restating the pain and problem*.

You've visited the customer's home and established they need a new boiler. As I've already explained, part of the quotation process is about asking lots of questions and finding out what the problem is and what inconvenience and disruption the problem is causing? Is the customer stressed? How are they inconvenienced? You've already identified the problems onsite and now it's time to reiterate them back to the customer. For example,

> "Mr and Mrs Pacquiao, thank you for inviting us into your home and allowing us to quote for your boiler replacement. Our understanding is your boiler has been down for a few days now and you have to have cold showers."

People are more motivated against the avoidance of pain than they are towards the motivation of gain.

Remind your customer of the pain points their problem is causing. People will usually not buy anything unless it avoids pain. There needs to be a reason as to why they're buying something and more often than not, it's the avoidance of pain. So, for a boiler replacement, the avoidance of pain might be they will no longer be cold, tired, stressed, irritated by the clanking noise, unable to bath the children at home, having to go to the gym for a shower, etc. This section may only need to be one sentence long. Use their words. Mirror their language.

Below, you will find some of the main reasons why someone would buy a new boiler along with example wording which you could use in a quote for each scenario:

- **A government grant may be available.**
  "Thank you for inviting us to your home and allowing us to quote for your boiler replacement. We understand you are eligible for a government grant which will fund the upgrade of your boiler. It is great to hear you want to make use of the grant available to you because otherwise, it would be a wasted opportunity."

- **A potential customer has just moved into a property and would like a new boiler with an extended warranty.**
  "Thank you for inviting us to your home and allowing us to quote for your boiler upgrade. Our understanding is you have recently moved into the property and you would like a brand-new boiler to compliment your new home. For extra peace of mind, your boiler is accompanied with an extended warranty which means you don't need to worry about any unexpected repair bills for the foreseeable future."

- **A home is undergoing renovations and the boiler needs to be relocated or upgraded.**
  "Thank you for inviting us into your home and allowing us to quote for a boiler replacement. Our understanding is the renovation works you're carrying out include a new bathroom and kitchen so you would like to upgrade and relocate the boiler. Having all the work done at the same time is certainly more cost-effective and will avoid disruption further down the line."

- **A potential customer has moved into a new property and wants a better boiler installed.**
  "Thank you for allowing us into your home to quote for a boiler replacement. Our understanding is you like the finer things in life

and would like a brand-new boiler installed. We also believe your home is your castle and so it would be a pleasure to assist you with this."

- **The existing boiler has been condemned.**
"Thank you for inviting us into your home and allowing us to quote for a boiler replacement. Our understanding is your boiler has been condemned, so you need to replace the boiler to get your house back to normality as quickly as possible."

- **The customer would like a combination boiler instead of a conventional system.**
"Thank you for inviting us into your home and allowing us to quote for a boiler replacement. We understand you currently have a conventional heating system and would like to upgrade to a combination boiler. We can confirm after speaking to you a combination boiler is suitable for your use and they're more efficient. Installing one will save you money on your future heating bills."

- **Looking to save money.**
"Thank you for inviting us into your home and allowing us to quote for a boiler replacement. Our understanding is you are looking to save money on your heating bills as they are currently extortionate. You feel like you're overpaying and having a new efficient combination boiler installed should save you some money."

The above examples clearly state reasons why a customer would want a new boiler and then has some further information as to what the result will look like for the customer. In fact, the pain is restated and then expanded on.

Usually, one of the above seven scenarios would be the reason for a boiler replacement. Therefore, if these are all included within the master quote template, you can simply delete the six irrelevant examples, meaning you have the main pain/problem left to include in the quote.

Hopefully, this results in a quick and reliable system for you to use time and time again.

Dear Mr and Mrs Foreman

Brand-new efficient Worcester Greenstar 25i boiler quote

Thank you for inviting us into your home and allowing us to quote for a boiler replacement. Our understanding is your boiler has been condemned, so you need to replace the boiler in order to get your house back to normality as quickly as possible.

CHAPTER 16

Take the pain away

In the previous chapter, I restated the pain points. In this section, I will now take the pain away by advising the customer how my company is going to fix the problem. For example, *"Don't worry, Best Boilers by Bill Limited are here to save the day. By installing a new boiler, we will bring normality back to your home. You will have hot water and heating again. This will be achieved by carrying out the following..."*

It might only be a couple of sentences (nothing too wordy), but it's a very important section. You have established the pain points and next, you need to highlight the transformation your solution will provide. The way you do this, during a boiler quotation, is to tell the customer the new appliance you're going to install will take away all the pain they have experienced, i.e. alleviate the problem.

Tailored to the customer

Get creative with this section... but tailor it to the individual customer. The more personal it is, the better because they will see that you're on their wavelength and have specifically tailored this to their situation. By making this section unique, you will come across as a company that has listened, understood the job in hand and genuinely want to help. People buy from people and the best way to achieve this is by mirroring people's language and words.

Highlight your business's qualifications

At this point you could also talk about your business's qualifications, for example, "Rest assured we're Gas Safe registered, so we fully comply with the up-to-date laws and regulations as dictated by our governing body, Gas Safe."

Reassuring the customer you're qualified and aligned with building regulations brings peace of mind. State which building regulations are being adhered to because this proves to the customer you have the expertise and will fill them with confidence in your business and the job in hand.

If other companies looking at the job aren't informing them they're qualified, or even what building regulations are being followed, then your quote is going to stand out when compared to your competition. The customer may not understand the industry jargon, so please do not go over the top on trying to impress the customer with fancy rules and regulations.

"Don't worry, Superb Plumbing and Heating are here to save the day. By installing a new boiler, you will have hot water and heating again and benefit from efficiency savings. This will be achieved by carrying out the works as stated in this quotation. Rest assured, we are Gas Safe registered and fully comply with the up-to-date laws and regulations as dictated by our governing body, Gas Safe (www.gassaferegister.co.uk)."

CHAPTER 17

Your bespoke quote

This section of the quote is where you inform the customer of everything included in their bespoke quote. Explain everything you're going to do to remedy your customer's problem in this section. This will cover the entire solution, the fix and nothing more. I suggest that you make the main body of the quote as concise as possible. If you want to go into more detail, then this should be included in the appendix and a reference made to it. Therefore, when informing the customer how you're going to take away their pain points, I recommend just sticking to a few paragraphs, bullet points or sections titles.

In this section. you also need to outline to the customer the exact work being undertaken. The reason I suggest limiting this section to a few paragraphs or titles is because not everyone wants the intricate details. Some customers just want to know that the work you're quoting for will fix the problem – i.e. go straight to the point. Customers who prefer knowing all the major details can obtain this information from the appendix. Subsequently, the quote should address both types of customer – the straight-to-the-point people and the detail hunters!

Selling the benefits

It is important to mention that customers buy benefits and not features. For example, carrying out a power flush is a feature, it is something which you're going to do. But what does this mean? Explain the benefits of this to the customer, for example:

"A power flush is a cleansing process which removes sludge built up inside your central heating system. A power flush cleans and maintains your central heating system to improve the amount of heat emitted from your radiators."

Inform your customers of the benefits of everything you do. Educate them about what you're doing, show them it is hard, that is requires a lot of skill, experience and will vastly benefit them. In return, customers will see you, your business and the industry in a much better light as well as having confidence when your price is what it is.

Turn features into benefits! When describing the elements that go into the boiler quote, it is important to explain what the benefits are of each feature. For example, "further to our recent visit, we have created this bespoke quotation to replace your current boiler and other stated appliances. We have briefly explained the works below. For, a more detailed explanation, please refer to the appendix."

"To supply and install a new Worcester Greenstar 25i boiler and horizontal flue along with:

- Magnetic filter
- Lime-scale reducer
- Pressure vessel
- Nonstandard pipework
- Insulation

The quoted price includes labour for a gas engineer, electrician, testing and commissioning."

To keep the main body of the quote lean, I suggest you append the key details. This is where you will turn the features into benefits. Here's a shed load from our example quote.

Appendix:

The following information explains your bespoke boiler installation.

Existing system

Turn off services to the existing system and drain. Disconnect existing boiler, hot and cold-water storage tanks and other heating system components as necessary and remove from site. Cut back any redundant pipework as required.

The boiler

Supply and install one Worcester Greenstar 25i combination boiler. Fit into position in the kitchen.

"Heating accounts for about 55% of what a household spends in a year on energy bills, so an efficient boiler can make a big difference to your bills."

Boiler flue

Supply and install a horizontal flue.

Please note: as this appliance is high efficiency, the flue will plume due to increased water content within the waste product.

Magnetic boiler filter

Supply one in-line magnetic filter and install into position on boiler return.

"A magnetic boiler filter is an attachment fitted directly to your central heating system. It collects various metallic particles, storing them safely so they don't form a sludge which can settle at the base of a boiler and cause major problems."

Lime-scale reducer

The boiler's cold water supply will have a lime-scale reducer fitted in order to reduce scale build up in the heat exchanger, therefore helping to prolong its life.

"The heat exchanger is an integral part of a boiler and can cost over £600 to replace."

Pressure expansion vessel

Supply and install one pressure expansion vessel complete with all associated gauges, valves and fittings. Install into primary return pipework.

Pipework

From the position of a new boiler, extend primary flow and return pipework as necessary and connect to existing boiler as required – to hot water cylinder position.

Insulation

All hot pipework connected to the hot water cylinder for a minimum of one metre or up to the point at which they are concealed and any new pipework in unheated areas, to be insulated.

In addition, any new pipework in unheated areas to be insulated.

"Insulating your hot water pipes reduces heat loss and can raise the water temperature 2°F-4°F hotter than uninsulated pipes can deliver, allowing you to lower your water temperature setting. You also won't have to wait

as long for hot water when you turn on a tap or showerhead, which helps conserve water."

Gas supply

From the position of the existing meter, which is the correct diameter to provide sufficient volume of gas, extend gas supply as necessary, connect to boiler and test for soundness.

Electric work

Wire up boiler and all associated controls, as necessary. Carry out electrical continuity bonding of the new heating system as required by current regulations.

Please note: this quotation does not allow for any other electrical work unless stated.

Ventilation grills

Supply and fit permanent ventilation grills as necessary to provide sufficient ventilation, in accordance with current regulations.

Testing and commissioning

Fill heating system and test. Refill adding anti-corrosion inhibitor. The system will be commissioned in compliance with Building Regulations X.

"An anti-corrosion inhibitor is a chemical compound, which when added to a heating system will decrease the corrosion rate of your pipes."

CHAPTER 18

Describe their options

It is important to give a customer at least three prices in one quote. I appreciate this may be a new concept, but please bear with me on this one while I explain. Often, when getting quotes for a boiler replacement, a person would get three quotes from three different plumbing and heating businesses. This is to get a feel for the price, the work involved and to ensure all quotes are in a ballpark figure, so they're not getting ripped off.

So, why don't you give the customer three quotes at once?

It saves them having to shop around and means you are more likely to get the business. The way to do this is to segment your customers. Place them into boxes! Offer more choice and add value. In life, there are three different shoppers:

The Value Shopper

They are purely interested in the price. They want a new boiler and they want it as cheap as possible. No frills – flies easyJet, shops at Lidl and cuts out coupons from the newspaper.

The Standard Shopper

Your run-of-the-mill, average person. Price is important but so is excellent service by a credible, qualified tradesperson who reassures them with total peace of mind. Shops at Tesco.

The Premium Shopper

Price isn't important to them. What is important is the ease of access and the functionality. They want to use a trusted brand, known for quality. They also want aftercare and support. These are your high-end luxury shoppers. Regarding a boiler, they'll probably want the most up-to-date boiler with the latest technology and gadgets. They're not shy about spending money to get luxury. They want the finer things in life. They probably fly with BA and shop at Waitrose.

I have produced a table (*see below*) which shows what each type of shopper would like in regard to their segment. This is so that you can see and consider the type of things that are important to them. The table will help you choose and then decide how you're going to describe a customer for each of your packages.

	Value	Standard	Premium
Price	Very important	Important	Less important
Qualified tradesman	Important	Very important	Very important
Credible service	Less important	Less important	Very important
Aftercare support	Less important	Less important	Very important
Trusted brand	Less important	Less important	Very important
Up-to-date technology	Less important	Less important	Very important
Quality	Less important	Less important	Very important

The value shopper is mainly after a cheap price and having a qualified tradesperson is also important. To a standard shopper, price is important but having a qualified tradesperson is very important. Meanwhile, for the premium shopper, price is less important, but having a qualified tradesperson, credible service, aftercare support, trusted brand, up-to-date technology and quality are all very important. Therefore, when describing your customer, these attributes must be considered.

Often, when plumbing and heating businesses provide a quote to a customer, they will give one price (see 'P2' on the graph below). Giving one option implies you are relying on the fact your quote is not above the customer's budget and that it's not too expensive, so that the customer doesn't buy, or too cheap so that you make no profit as a business. By offering the customer three different prices (the value shopper, the standard shopper and the premium shopper), you cover all angles. The easiest way to explain this is by referring to a graph often used in economic studies to explain supply and demand.

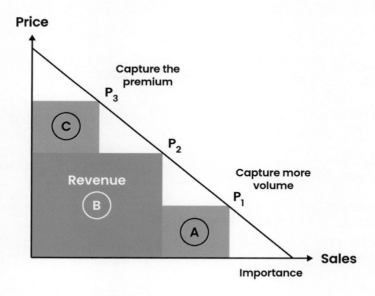

This graph tells us, as the price goes up, the quantity of sales goes down and vice versa. As the price for a boiler goes down, the quantity sold increases. Subsequently, as the price for a boiler installation increases, the quantity of boiler installations sold by a plumbing and heating installation company decreases. The boilers sold will be at premium prices with good gross profit margins, as illustrated by 'P3' on the graph and in the following numerical description. If five premium boilers sold at £3000 = £15000 or 10 value boilers sold at £1500 = £15000, therefore turnover is the same in both examples. However, the premium plumbing and heating firm may have a higher gross profit margin. And, as the quantity sold is lower, you will not be overworked; this could be a high-end, premium, boutique company of plumbers and gas engineers.

As the price comes down, the quantity sold goes up. Consequently, the cheaper the boiler installation quote, in theory, the more boiler quotes will be accepted. This is stacking them high, selling them cheap and often leads to being overloaded with work for very little minimum return. This is a the low-margin work/burnout model as illustrated by 'P1' on the graph. Therefore, do you want to be a premium plumbing and heating company or a budget high-volume plumbing and heating company?

When you offer 'one quote, one option, one price' to a customer, the price a customer accepts would be 'P2'. From a standard, run-of-the-mill plumbing and heating company's perspective, you don't want to be too expensive, so the customer doesn't buy and you don't want to be too cheap, resulting in no or little profit and money being left on the table. Never leave money on the table!

However, all too often, a run-of-the-middle, 'P2', average market price is presented to a customer. And, my point to you would be, when going for a run-of-the-middle pricing strategy (P2), a customer might not have bought from you because you're too expensive. They may have bought at a price 'P1' as opposed to price 'P2' so, therefore, you're missing out on business because you haven't offered a cheaper alternative to the run-of-the-mill quote. In addition, you might have sold a boiler to a customer at 'P2' because you only offer one price, but they could be a Premium Shopper and would have been willing to go to a much higher price as seen on the graph at point 'P3'. Let's say you've sold a boiler at price 'P2', but the customer would have paid price 'P3', therefore, you've left money on the table! Again... *don't* leave money on the table!

Always offer three different prices

It makes no sense to offer one price because you're either leaving money on the table or you're not selling the maximum number of boilers that you might sell. By giving one single price, the likelihood it is the exact price the customer will pay is almost zero. Therefore, always offer customers three different price options and hedge your bets! These options need to take into account the:

- **Value Shopper** – Mr/Mrs Budget. All they're interested in is the price.

- **Standard Shopper** – Mr/Mrs Average. Price is important but so is good customer service and a quality tradesperson.

- **Premium Shopper** – Mr/Mrs Luxury. Their focus is high-end.

A simple accounting equation – 'total revenue = price x quantity sold'. If you compare 'P3' to 'P1' below, you will see the shaded area is revenue.

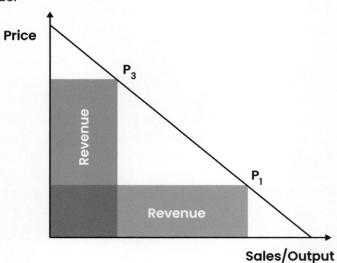

Guess what?... revenue is the same at both points! But in this model, note that 'P3' has installed less boilers, therefore, gross profit will be higher. I need to stress this is only a model and has been used to prove how offering one price point for something is never a good idea.

Target the premium shopper

Being cheap is not good, you owe it to yourself to target the premium shopper and charge higher prices for better gross-profit margins. I also need to stress that by going for the premium shopper, you will also attract other costs associated with being a premium company, such as new vans, higher advertising and marketing costs, experienced engineers, high-end office and administration staff offering the best customer service, up-to-date technology, etc.

An added point would be that you cannot be cheap and offer a high-end service as your bottom line, profit won't be present... you will be bending over backwards for a pittance. Don't bend over backwards for pittance! Pick a path and stick to it, being budget or high-end – just don't mix the two as your marketing material and image won't be aligned.

To reiterate, it's often the case when someone needs something new, (like a big household purchase or building works, etc) they will get three quotes from three different businesses. The reason people do this is so they can get a feel for what the cost of a job is going to be. As this is such common practice, I recommend you give a potential customer three prices; three options in your quotation.

Three boiler options

In this section of the quote, you will learn how to describe the three different options you are offering. To ease you into this new concept, the three different options could mean three different boilers with three different prices:

1. **A high-end premium boiler** (e.g. a Worcester Bosch)

2. **A standard/mid-range boiler** (e.g. a Vaillant)

3. **A value boiler** (e.g. an Alpha).

Even better, you could offer three levels of service and three different packages. First, for the value shopper, you offer a basic 'fix only', where you only replace the boiler with nothing else (no inflight meals!). The second, is a more standard service where you could offer more add-on features and benefits, compared to the value package. The third option would go even further and offer services, such as: aftercare, guarantees, warranties (more leg room and the all bells and whistles package!).

Now, it has already been established you need to give customers options. Explain those options to the customer and understand which type of customer might be attracted to each option. I would suggest you get creative with your option titles. Don't call them 'the value shopper, the standard shopper and the premium shopper' as this may have negative connotations; instead, perhaps try the following:

• Bronze, Silver and Gold

• Essentials, Premium and Premium-Plus packages

• Essentials, Advanced and Premium packages

• 3-Star, 4-Star and 5-Star

When describing the type of customer an option/package is designed for, it's important to link this back to what is important to a customer segment. The following examples illustrate what could be used:

Essentials package/Bronze/3-Star
This boiler quotation is for the more budget-cautious household, happy to miss out on the added extras but instead, just want a

basic boiler replacement. Rest assured, we promise to deliver great workmanship, attention to detail, and the customer care we are known for.

Premium package/Silver/4-Star/Advanced

This is our most popular option and is for households that want to go beyond the essentials needed to replace the boiler. You will receive the best aftercare and we will also carry out a power flush of your entire system to ensure sludge is removed and efficiency is maintained.

Premium Plus package/Gold/5-Star

This is the best option for tech-savvy property owners who enjoy the finer things in life. You want the best products, the best add-ons and the best aftercare for complete peace of mind. We'll even look at the rest of your system while onsite so you can rest assured knowing everything is taken care of.

I mentioned earlier you can offer different boilers. The way these fit into your quote uses the same segmentations. The Worcester Bosch boiler could be for the premium household, the Vaillant could be for the standard household, and the Alpha boiler could be for the value-budget conscious household.

Again, when you're describing your customer, break it down like as I did above. For example, *"The Worcester Bosch boiler is a prestigious boiler. It's well respected in the marketplace for performance and excellent customer care and service. We can also offer X years manufacturer's warranty"*. Then, describe the type of customer who may go for the Vaillant and the budget-range, Alpha, clearly mentioning the warranty period.

Segment your customers and explain each in detail so the customer can read and relate to a segment. If a segment fits them personally, and clearly describes the type of customer, then they will buy.

CHAPTER 19

Set out everything you do

In the previous section, I explained the need to provide three options in a quote to provide the customer with choices. By giving the customer choices, you're not selling to them, they're choosing to buy. I am just going to repeat that... you're not selling to them... they're choosing to buy and how much to spend.

If you can get your head around this, it's a very powerful concept. Instead of putting together a single-price quote, by presenting it as a cheaper or similar figure to what they were expecting to pay, or what they have been quoted by a competitor for a boiler replacement, you're letting them choose how much they want to pay, but in exchange for a varying degree of service, add-ons and features. You're covering all angles even though you don't yet know what type of shopper they are (value, standard or premium). As mentioned, you're hedging your bets!

Even if you think you know what price point they're at from the home survey, keep your options open... many people plead poverty in order to get the best deal they can, when in fact they have the money and are quite willing to pay for quality products and services from a reputable company.

Brainstorming a bespoke boiler installation

Now we have established how important the three-tier quote is, and what is important to each type of shopper, the next stage is to present what it includes in each segment on offer. The best way to do this is to brainstorm everything which you can possibly do for a boiler replacement installation. I would suggest you sit down with your team (or by yourself if you're a sole trader) and think of all the added benefits you can offer to improve, enhance, and add value to a boiler replacement. List everything you can offer and any additional add-ons.

Please remember the previous section of the quote (*see* Chapter 17 Your bespoke quote) which lists all the essential elements you need in order to install a new boiler. All the essential elements have already been considered and will be included in the quote regardless. Therefore, in this section we are purely focusing on the enhancements, taking a step further and adding value.

Here are some suggestions:

- Bleed the radiators
- Boiler covered by the manufacturer's warranty
- Boiler installation date guarantee
- Carry out a power flush
- Carry out a water test
- Check and review the rest of the system
- Chemical flush of the system
- Clean and tidy promise
- Dispose of old parts
- Drain down the system
- Easy payment options
- Aftercare from our call centre
- Full explanation of the new boiler and how to use it
- Full system set up to your requirements
- Fully-qualified engineers performing the installation
- Install modern TRVs
- Onsite aftercare from a supervisor
- Outside tap
- Routine service on the boiler's birthday
- Smart controls

- System upgrade recommendations
- The answer to the wish question (*see* Chapter 8 Scoping out the work).

So, now what I need to do is put each item into one of four categories. The reason I say four categories is, other than the three we have discussed (value, standard and premium), you'll also find you can offer services which may not fit within one of the three packages. Therefore, this needs to be added in a different part of the quote – i.e. 'add-ons' or 'optional extras'.

As a further note, the reason we have four different categories is because it's very important you don't include something in a package which doesn't relate to the customer or type of customer. For example, you've established you have a value shopper. All the value shopper wants is a boiler replacement at a good price. If you then present to your value shopper, a smart control, this won't appeal to them because you're presenting something they simply don't want or need. By adding something to a package which doesn't meet the buyer's needs, they won't buy because it isn't relatable and you could lose credibility for not understanding their needs. Therefore, you should present the quote across three different tiers but also have an add-on section where anything which doesn't fit can be included. This comes back to *'letting the customer buy'* concept; they will buy if the package meets their particular needs, so don't alienate them by ramming something down their throat.

Most items included in the value package will then also be in the standard and premium packages. Most items in the standard package will also be in the premium package. If it doesn't fit in a package, then it's an add-on or optional extra.

Upon getting your list, you can categorise each feature into one of the four options, based on what is important to that segment. Below, is an example table of the four different categories a feature could be placed:

Bespoke quotation (as stated above with further information in the appendix)	Value package
Easy payment options	Value package
Boiler installation date guarantee	Value package
Clean and tidy promise	Value package
Fully qualified engineers performing the installation	Value package
Drain down the system	Value package
Bleed the radiators	Value package
Full explanation of the new boiler and how to use it	Value package
Boiler covered by the manufacturers warranty	Value package
Chemical flush of the system	Value package only
Carry out a power flush	Standard and premium packages only
Carry out a water test	Standard package
Dispose of old parts	Standard package
Aftercare from our call centre	Standard package
Check and review the rest of the system	Premium package
System upgrade recommendations	Premium package
Full system set up to your requirements	Premium package
Onsite aftercare from a supervisor	Premium package
Routine service on the boilers' birthday	Premium package
The answer to the wish question (see Chapter 8 Scoping out the work)	Premium package
Smart controls	Optional extra
Outside tap	Optional extra
Install modern TRVs	Optional extra

Voila, you now have your packages!

You now have a complete list of features for a boiler replacement. I have placed the features into one of four different packages. Taking this concept further still, the unique features could be elegantly presented into a simple tick-list table, with ticks and crosses to show what is and isn't included in a package.

Going back to the previous example where you're offering value, standard and premium packages, I suggest you present this to customers with a clear visual tick-list table. With this approach, the customer will have a visual guide to what is in each package as well as what is excluded from each package. Below, is an example of such a table.

Feature	Value	Standard	Premium	Optional Extra
Bespoke quotation (as stated above with further information in the appendix)	✓	✓	✓	
Easy payment options	✓	✓	✓	
Boiler installation date guarantee	✓	✓	✓	
Clean and tidy promise	✓	✓	✓	
Fully qualified engineers performing the installation	✓	✓	✓	
Drain down the system	✓	✓	✓	
Bleed the radiators	✓	✓	✓	
Full explanation of the new boiler and how to use it	✓	✓	✓	

Feature	Value	Standard	Premium	Optional Extra
Boiler covered by the manufacturer's warranty	X years	X years	X years	
Chemical flush of the system	✓	–	–	
Carry out a power flush	–	✓	✓	
Carry out a water test	✗	✓	✓	
Dispose of old parts	✗	✓	✓	
Aftercare from our call centre	✗	✓	✓	
Check and review the rest of the system	✗	✗	✓	
System upgrade recommendations	✗	✗	✓	
Full system set up to your requirements	✗	✗	✓	
Onsite aftercare from a supervisor	✗	✗	✓	
Routine service on the boilers' birthday	✗	✗	✓	
The answer to the wish question (see Chapter 8 Scoping out the work)	✗	✗	✓	
Smart controls				✓
Outside tap				✓
Install modern TRVs				✓

By presenting this table, you're showing the customer what they get if they go for the value package, a bespoke boiler quote. That basically means, what the customer has asked for is all they're going to get, nothing additional, the bog-standard stuff and no inflight meals! In the next stage, the standard shopper will get the bespoke boiler quote, but they'll also get some additional features and support. Keep adding on features so the customer gets more than your value offer. By giving them more features, benefits and controls, you're creating a new package. By creating a new package, you can then quote a higher price. If the customer's willingness to pay is higher than the value shopper price, then they'll go for the standard (assuming this meets their needs).

After this, you need to add even more value – more services, products and offerings to the premium buyer. This is a very powerful technique because it shows the customer what is included and what is not. It has an element of FOMO (fear of missing out). What I mean is, if someone has gone for the value package, they know what they're getting, but they can also see what they're not getting and, therefore, what they are missing out on. Understanding what they would be missing out on may lead them towards the next tier up. They don't want to miss out on all the extra features which are available, especially if you're granting customers their wish list! They want ticks not crosses!

I've mentioned before when you present your quote, the content needs to be clear and concise. You don't want to overload it with information because some people will just glance over it. By having a lean quote which isn't too wordy, you're appealing to customers who don't require the detail. That being said, you don't want to alienate those who do require the detail. Therefore, I suggest you have an appendix for each package feature provided in the quote, where you'll list out the benefits of each. To illustrate this, please refer to the appendix example section below where each feature has a detailed explanation of what they entail exactly.

Easy payment options

We accept cash, cheques, BACS, credit and debit cards. We don't charge extra for credit cards. Payment is required when an option has been selected and any add-ons, this is to secure your selection so we know how to proceed with your request and to book in an installation date. We also offer finance, via a third party.

Boiler installation date guarantee

Once we have booked in your installation, we guarantee we will show up. If we don't, then we will give you £x – this is our 'show up guarantee'. (*See* T&Cs online)

Clean and tidy promise

We will use dust sheets wherever required and promise to fully clean up after ourselves. If you're not satisfied with our cleaning, then we will give you £x – this is our 'clean up guarantee'. (*See* T&Cs online)

Fully-qualified engineers performing the installation

All our engineers are fully-qualified tradespeople who have dedicated their careers to being qualified in gas, oil, LPG, electrics and renewable technologies.

Drain down the system

In order to replace the boiler, the water in the system often needs to be drained.

Bleed the radiators

As part of the boiler replacement and to ensure the heating system is fully tested, we will bleed the radiators; this is the reverse effect of the drain down (mentioned above). This means all excess air in the system will be removed. This will be performed after the boiler has been installed.

Full explanation of the new boiler and how to use it

We will show you what we have replaced and explain the controls, providing a full explanation of how to use your new appliances.

Boiler covered by the manufacturer's warranty

Manufacturers offer a standard x-year warranty or x-year warranty if a filter is installed giving you added peace of mind. Please be aware your boiler may need to be serviced periodically to maintain the manufacturer's warranty. We also offer a boiler service plan.

Chemical flush of the system

Inhibitors remove sludge, scale and debris from the existing central heating system to restore heating efficiency and eliminate boiler noise. The inhibitor we use is a non-hazardous product which is compatible with all metals commonly used in heating systems.

Carry out a power flush

A power flush is a cleansing process which removes sludge build up inside your central heating system. A power flush is an ideal solution to clean and maintain your central heating system and improve the amount of heat permitted from your radiators.

Carry out a water test

We will test the water in your system for contaminants, reporting back the findings and a resolution if required.

Dispose of old parts

We will take away all old parts and dispose of them in an environmentally-friendly manner. Any packaging will be recycled.

Aftercare from our call centre

In the weeks after the boiler installation, our knowledgeable call centre team will ring you to ensure everything is running as it should be. Any questions will be answered and addressed.

Check and review the rest of the system

Our trained engineers will review the rest of your heating and hot water system to ensure there are no leaks, faults, damage or problems. We will look at your heating system through thermal heat-seeking goggles to identify anomalies. This is an extremely valuable service to ensure your heating system is working properly.

Customers can benefit from having a thermal inspection done. Heat-seeking goggles detect temperature by recognising and capturing different levels of infrared light (invisible to the naked eye) which are felt as heat when the intensity is high enough. This valuable service allows engineers to detect thermal defects, heat losses and air leakages and then determine whether better insulation is needed. The technique can also be used to ensure insulation has been installed properly and to check the effectiveness of your overall home insulation.

System upgrade recommendations

While reviewing your system our engineers will recommend:

- New technologies to get the best out of your system.
- Any energy-saving tips and tricks, saving you money.
- Other ways to improve your current heating and hot water system and discuss any such requirements.

Full system set up to your requirements

The buttons on the boiler and thermostats can be confusing. Our engineers will fully customise the heating system to your personal preference. For example, the radiators can be set to automatically come on at 7am and turn off at 10pm. The choice is yours.

Onsite aftercare from a supervisor

In the weeks after the boiler installation, a supervisor will revisit your property to ensure everything is running as it should be. Any questions can be answered and addressed.

Routine service on the boiler's birthday

We will attend your property the following year to service the boiler. This is a requirement to validate the manufacturer's warranty. (*See* T&Cs online)

Answering the wish question (*see* Chapter 8 Scoping out the work)

If you asked your customer the question about granting them a wish and this is doable, then include their response in this section. By including it in the premium section of the quote, you're 'nudging' your customer to go for this package.

The following information explains what is included in the Essentials, Premium and Premium Plus packages:

Easy payment options

We accept cash, cheques, BACS, credit and debit cards. We don't charge extra for credit cards. Payment is required when an option has been selected, including the price of any add-ons. This is to secure your selection and enables us to secure an installation date.
We also offer finance, via a third party.

Boiler installation date guarantee

Once we have booked in your installation, we guarantee we will show up. If we do not, then we will give you £50 – this is our 'Show-Up Guarantee'. (*See* T&Cs online)

Clean-up guarantee

We will use dust sheets wherever required and promise we will fully clean up after ourselves. We guarantee we will clean up. If you feel we have not fully cleaned up after ourselves, then we will give you £50 – this is our 'Clean-Up Guarantee'. (*See* T&Cs online)

Fully-qualified engineers performing the installation

All of our engineers are fully-qualified tradespeople who have dedicated years of their lives to be qualified in gas, oil, LPG, electrics and renewables technologies.

Drain down the system

In order to replace the boiler, the water in the system often needs to be drained.

Bleed the radiators

As part of the boiler replacement and to ensure the heating system is fully tested, we will bleed the radiators; this is the reverse effect of the drain down, mentioned above. This means all excess air in the system will be removed. This will be performed after the boiler has been installed.
Full explanation of the new boiler and how to use it

We will show you what we have replaced, explain the new controls and fully explain how to use your new appliances.

Boiler covered by the manufacturer's warranty

Manufacturers offer a standard x-year warranty or x-year warranty if a filter is installed giving you added peace of mind. Please be aware your boiler may need to be serviced periodically to maintain the manufacturer's warranty. We also offer a boiler service plan.

Chemical flush of the system

Inhibitors remove sludge, scale and debris from the existing central heating system to restore heating efficiency and eliminate boiler noise. The inhibitor we use is a non-hazardous product compatible with all metals commonly used in heating systems.

The following information explains what is included in the Premium and Premium Plus package:

Carry out a power flush

A power flush is a cleansing process which removes sludge build up inside your central heating system. A power flush is an ideal solution to clean and maintain your central heating system to improve the amount of heat permitted from your radiators.

Carry out a water test

We will test the water in your system for contaminants, reporting back to you the findings and a resolution if required.

Dispose of old parts

We will take away all old parts and dispose of them in an environmentally-friendly manner and recycle any packaging.

Aftercare from our call centre

In the weeks after the boiler installation, our knowledgeable call centre team will ring you to ensure everything is running as it should be. Any questions will be answered and addressed.

The following information explains what is included in the Premium Plus package only:

Check and review the rest of the system

Our trained engineers will review the rest of your heating and hot water system to ensure there are no leaks, faults, damage, or problems. We will look at your heating system through thermal heat-seeking goggles to identify anomalies. This is an extremely valuable service in ensuring your heating system is working properly. Customers can benefit from having a thermal inspection done. Heat-seeking goggles detect temperature by recognising and capturing different levels of infrared light (invisible to the naked eye) which are felt as heat when the intensity is high enough. This valuable service allows engineers to detect thermal defects, heat losses and air leakages and then determine whether better insulation is needed. The technique can also be used to ensure insulation has been installed properly and to check the effectiveness of your overall home insulation.

System upgrade recommendations

While reviewing your system, our engineers will recommend:

- New technologies to get the best out of your system.
- Any energy-saving tips and tricks, saving you money.
- Discuss your current heating and hot water requirements.

Full system set up to your requirements

The buttons on the boiler and thermostats can be confusing. Our engineer will fully customise the heating system to your preference. For example, they can set the radiators to come on at 7am and turn off at 10am. The choice is yours.

Onsite aftercare from a supervisor

In the weeks after the boiler installation, a supervisor will revisit your property to ensure everything is running as it should be. Any questions will be answered and addressed.

Routine service on the boiler's birthday

We will attend your property the following year to service the boiler. This is a requirement to validate the manufacturer's warranty. (*See* T&Cs online)

CHAPTER 20

State your prices

It's very important your prices are correct when quoting for work. There are two parties in the quote – the seller and the buyer. Both parties have got different goals, different agendas and want different outcomes.

First, the seller (i.e. you), hopes to get the maximum price from the customer (we often call this the 'maximum willingness to pay'). The buyer, meanwhile, wants to get the best deal out of the seller (perceiving this to mean the 'cheapest price'). Actually, it's very different. What the best deal means is 'profit on the deal' or the 'perceived profit on the deal', which I will explain.

For now, let's concentrate on you, the seller. Work out your total business operational costs (fixed overheads) and your break-even point (the point where you're not making a profit or a loss). No-one goes into business to break-even. You need to make profit to pay the bills, feed the children, have a nice car, go on holiday and to live the lifestyle you choose.

Once you have your break-even point, most people work on a mark-up; their day-rate and how much they want to get paid on top of the break-even point. This is, therefore, going to be the seller's minimum price. After you factor in your costs – labour, materials and expenditure – you know you can't charge for a boiler installation below x amount. If you do, you're making a loss and making a loss is not sustainable. There is no point being in business if you're making a loss. You now have your 'seller's minimum price' – you can't sell at anything beneath this price.

(Please note: this a very simple overview of obtaining your minimum seller's price. I could write another book around how to charge your magic price, but this is outside the remit of *The Quote Handbook*!)

Next, let's focus on the buyer (i.e. the customer). A buyer has got a maximum willingness to pay, this is known as a 'reservation price'. There are only four reasons a customer will not buy from you:

1. There isn't enough value.
2. They can't see the value.
3. They can't afford you.
4. They can buy it cheaper elsewhere.

I want to break these down and show how producing an excellent quality quote, with all the distinct elements explored in this book, can eliminate these four reasons:

1. **There isn't enough value.** *The Quote Handbook* is about adding value. I'm showing the customer what they're getting and then presenting a price. I'm offering them a bespoke boiler quotation. Besides that, they're also getting the features and benefits as stated in the value, standard or premium options. What this does, is build perceived value in the customer's eyes; everything which they will get is stated and presented to the customer. By producing a detailed in-depth quote, the next point is alleviated.

2. **They can't see the value.** By clearly presenting to the customer what they're getting for their money, it is about being transparent, in black and white. Showing how the customer will gain a profit on the deal (i.e. the amount of value being added to the property less the cost of the installation) will help the customer understand the value of the job.

3. **They can't afford you.** If that's the case, you can go back and work with the customer so they can afford you. Later in *The Quote Handbook*, I talk about 'behaviour rewards' whereby you

can offer the customer something in return for something they can do for you. You can exchange a cheaper price for a referral or a testimonial. It could even be something like the customer will dispose of all the waste, therefore cutting down your waste-disposal costs and saving you a bit of time. Get creative! If you really want to work for a customer and they really want you to do the work, don't drop your price to a point where you aren't making any profit, drop it slightly so you adapt the work and the business gets something out of it. If a customer just flat out can't afford you, then you need to look at your marketing. Why have you attracted a customer you do not cater for? For example, are you a premium heating and plumbing company who has been contacted by a value shopper? Reassess your marketing and ensure you only go to potential customers suited to your ideal customers. Do not waste that £160 on a quote that will go nowhere *(as mentioned on page 19)*.

4. **They can buy it cheaper elsewhere.** If they can get it cheaper elsewhere, it is just one of those things in business. You can't win every customer. You can't please everyone and, unfortunately, there are going to be cheap inferior plumbing and heating businesses out there who are bending over backwards for pittance or busting a gut for small profit margins. Trust me, those sorts of tradespeople don't stay around for long. If a customer can get it cheaper elsewhere, let the other company take a loss on that job and bid the customer farewell!

Another point I need to explain is a customer will buy from you straight away if they see a profit in the deal. I've explained how to build up value. If you then present your price, and they were expecting a price which is much higher than one of your three offerings, they're going to buy from you straight away because they are seeing a profit in the deal. Just to reiterate, a customer will buy from you if they see profit in the deal. Even if the profit is perceived profit *(see* Chapter 12 Anchor). Their potential profit on the deal is achieved by installing a new boiler, which in turn, could potentially add £12,720 to the current value of their property.

When we go through the tick-list technique with the customer and we clearly explain everything they're getting in the package (and present a total price for the package), if a customer looks at the standard option and says *"wow, a power flush and you'll dispose of the old parts, plus a full explanation of how to use the boiler settings is included"*… all these add-ons are an extra price to the deal. If the customer perceives the value of each feature is more than you are charging them, they will see a profit in the deal. If there's a profit in the deal, the customer is going to buy.

Please note: I don't know anyone that will go *"wow, a power flush and you'll dispose of the old parts, plus a full explanation of how to use the boiler settings is included"* but hopefully you understand my point!

I hope this explains the customer's willingness to pay and how presenting your quotes, in the manner described in *The Quote Handbook*, will help your plumbing and heating company to stand out. Your aim is to be completely different to your competition so that your quote is not comparable at all. Clearly showing the customer how your business goes many steps further than your cheaper competitors and are completely transparent with the job in hand.

More pricing techniques

Normally, when someone is producing a quote, they put the price right at the end. Consequently, what happens is they produce a beautiful quotation where they explain to the customer all of the different features and benefits, etc, then right at the end of it is the price. That tends to be the stopping point for the customer and the deciding factor.

What I suggest you do is state the price or prices in the middle of the quotation. This is so the customer doesn't get distracted by the prices. List the features, then show the price options. You can then explain what they will get for the price in more detail and what the benefit of those features are. The price isn't the last focus if it is laid out in this way.

The whole point of a quote is to deliver a product and service to the customer they already want. The price is an off-shoot of that. If someone needs a new boiler, then they need a new boiler. It is going to happen regardless because they need heating and hot water, essential human amenities. Therefore, mix the prices in the middle so it is not their final thought.

Stating your price and payment options

This section of the quote is where you present your price and your payment options. First, I would always suggest you get paid in full for a boiler installation prior to starting the job. Failing that, then anything between 50% to 99% should be obtained. Explaining you require a deposit upfront to cover the material costs usually sways customers to agree. There are ways to get creative with obtaining deposits and you can also use pricing psychology to make the price seem smaller by using the following techniques.

For example, let's say for your standard package a boiler replacement is £3,000.00. Instead of saying to the customer "this is going to cost you £3000" how about you say to them "it's just three simple payments of £1000".

Even though it's the same price, the latter seems less. You can use your payment terms to get creative making the price appear smaller. I also recommend playing about with how the numbers are presented. For example, £3,000.00 seems longer than £3000 even though they're the exact same price. People tend to read numbers in their head and the longer the glance, the longer the perceived amount. Therefore, consider omitting commas and the pence or decimal points.

You can also play around with the payment terms to make your premium package seem cheaper. For example:

Value: £3000 + VAT

Standard: three payments of £1200 + VAT

Premium: five payments of £840 + VAT

In practice, what you're doing is offering less payment terms for the customers who want the value package, but by doing that you also make your premium package seem less expensive.

The total costs in these examples are as follows:

Value: £3000 + VAT

Standard: three payments of £1200 + VAT = £3600 + VAT

Premium: five payments of £840 + VAT = £4200 + VAT

I would also avoid rounding up figures. Instead of offering a price of £3000, offer them a price of £2987. Research has shown when prices are displayed as round figures in the hundreds or thousands, they feel made up and plucked out of thin air. It seems less considered and calculated than a price of say £2987. An obscure number will reassure the customer different elements have been added together to build the total price and the price is purely unique for them. Research also reveals that people are less inclined to haggle a non-round number ending in 0 or 5.

Always ask for a deposit

It's very important you ask for a deposit as standard. Whilst it may feel a little uncomfortable at first, I guarantee your customers won't question it. They'll accept it as your trading terms.

I've based *The Quote Handbook* on a boiler replacement, but let's say you're installing a boiler, bathroom and all the associated pipework and appliances for a new-build house. The schedule of works is going to span more than three months. Match your price to the timescale.

For example, *"every Friday we will raise an invoice for £1,538 for 13 weeks".* That will seem cheaper than saying the entire job will cost £19,994. Break up the payments to compliment the timescale of work due to be carried out.

And, always make it easy for the customer to pay. This could be something as simple as saying, for example, *"we offer the following payment options: BACS bank transfer (sort code xx-xx-xx / account number xxxxxxx), cash, cheque, credit or debit cards."*

If a customer wishes to pay by card, ensure you have a Process Data Quickly (PDQ) machine at the ready or someone available to process the payment over the phone in your office. Also, if you prefer to be paid via direct debit, inform the customer this is your preferred payment method, especially if you're offering payments in instalments, make it a term of your business. GoCardless is a popular product used for collecting direct debits.

If you offer boiler finance, this is also the section where you'll need to inform customers you offer this service and insert your standard wording from the third-party finance company. This section of the quote is *very* important. It's the reason most of us go to work each day – to get paid!

You need to make it as easy as possible for the customer to pay you. The way you do that is by describing the different payment options. Make them clear. In summary, try to chunk down your price as much as possible or chunk it up if you're presenting the value package to discourage this option.

Calculating the price

I have explained how to state the price, the importance of requesting an upfront deposit and recommended payment options, but here are some effective ways to calculate the price.

In practice, you would often:

1. Put together a materials list for a boiler replacement, add a mark-up.

2. Work out how many days and engineers it would take to do the job at their going rates.

These two points combined should be the price you present to a potential customer. For example, the boiler and associated ancillaries may come to £1,200. Your mark-up could then be 40%, totalling £1,680.

Let's say your day-rate for an engineer is £400 and it's a one-day job. Therefore, you would quote the customer £2,080 + VAT.

I've made it extremely clear of the need to give the customer three options. In fact, we need to take this concept of pricing one step further to account for the options. And, using the table which I have previously used, we can price up each line.

Feature	Value	Standard	Premium	Price
Your bespoke boiler quote	✓	✓	✓	£2080
Carry out a power flush	✗	✓	✓	£450
Onsite aftercare from a supervisor	✗	✗	✓	£150
Routine gas service	✗	✗	✓	£70
	£2080	£2530	£2750	

You can now provide the customer with three different options and quickly. All the information from this table should be on a template (don't show the customer the different price points you have added, as displayed on the far right).

You have your base price which would also be the value package price. Then, give each line a set price for the feature being offered, allowing you to easily add up a price for the standard and premium packages.

To quickly provide a customer three different options, all you would need to do is add up a materials list for each job which will be the bespoke boiler quoted price. As long as you know your sales price for each service offering (e.g. how much you sell a typical power flush for depending on the property) you can then deliver three prices, quickly and cover all three shoppers (value, standard and premium).

As you get more familiar with offering three different prices, options and packages, you can insert a line into your template and add in the price, working out which package the product fits into.

Upgrade and nudge

You will notice in the above example, the difference in price of each package is not equal. The premium package is closer to the standard package (i.e. £2,750-£2,530=£220), as compared to the value and standard difference (i.e. £2,530-£2,080=£450). People who may be a standard shopper will look at the price of the premium package and think for a little extra money, I could benefit from everything!

This is called the 'upgrade and nudge'. If the standard shopper goes for the premium, they've gone from spending £2,530 to £2,750 or an additional £220, which is an 8.7% increase in spend. Now extrapolate this 8.7% increase in boiler sales across your entire business, what would you do with this additional sales revenue and additional profit?

Price order and the anchor

In the western world, we read from left to right. Therefore, I would suggest you present the order of packages on the quote from the most expensive to the cheapest. By seeing the premium expensive price first, sets a precedence in the buyer's mind. It could be "wow, that's expensive!", their heart-rate will increase, but then they read on to the standard and value prices, therefore, decreasing their heart-rate and making them content in the buying process.

An alternative to the upgrade and nudge concept is the 'anchor' (*see* Chapter 12 Anchor). The premium package could be used as an anchor to get your customers to buy the standard package. And, using the above example, I could price the premium package at £3277. This is a big difference when compared to the standard being £2530 and even more when compared to the value being £2080. This number sets the stage and now both the standard and value prices seem reasonable, therefore, tempting your customers onto the standard package.

Please note: if you sell all of your packages at the premium level, your premium price is too low. If you sell no value packages, then you are way too expensive overall. In life, 20% of people are value shoppers, 70% are standard shoppers and 10% are premium shoppers. Subsequently, you could set your sales targets on this if you are a run-of-the-mill plumbing and heating company. If you are a premium plumbing and heating company, and have structured your business as such, then the above figure/percentage splits would be more geared towards the premium buyers. And, vice versa, if you have structured your business to be a value plumbing and heating company.

Track, monitor and measure your pricing results, tweak changes and be flexible. If something isn't working or doesn't sit right, then try something new. I have given a few different pricing concepts here; it is down to you to adopt what you feel would work for a particular situation.

I am setting out the tools to open your eyes to new ways of preparing a boiler quotation. If something works perfectly, and brings in significant results, roll it out to your entire business!

The Quote Handbook focuses on a boiler replacement, but using the concepts and techniques I am sharing will empower you with the know-how to use these teachings for other products and services, such as: bathroom refurbishments, cylinder replacements and other routine services and installation works. If you can brainstorm how to add value to a particular product or service, you will be amazed what you come up with, present to a customer and then ultimately deliver.

Fast track service

An additional way to increase the price is to offer a 'fast track service'. This is where if the boiler is condemned or isn't working, you can explain to the customer you usually operate on a three weeks' notice schedule but because it's an urgent situation, you can offer the engineers overtime and weekend work to fit them in. This will be an additional charge because you must pay the engineers an additional wage in order to compensate them for working out-of-hours.

Get smart and creative when pricing up for the customer, but always make it transparent. Often, pricing is seen as a vulgar topic which gets frowned upon when spoken about. But, the price of your products and services is vital to being in business and staying in business. Be confident in your pricing and terms and stick to your guns. If a customer doesn't like your prices, offer 'behaviour rewards' (explained later). Alternatively, walk away.

If you are a truly skilled and honest tradesperson who cares about your customers, then please don't see these pricing techniques as ways to trick your customers into buying. If your boiler quotation solution is the best solution for a customer, then you can use pricing psychology techniques positively. The customer will benefit from your service and the only way they can do that is to buy from you. The techniques explored here put you onto a better pedestal for helping more customers. At the end of the experience, the customer's needs would be fulfilled, and they would have bought from you at a price point they're comfortable with.

EXAMPLE

Feature	Premium Plus package	Premium package	Essentials package
Bespoke quotation (as stated above with further information in the appendix)	✓	✓	✓
Easy payment options	✓	✓	✓
Boiler installation date guarantee	✓	✓	✓
Clean and tidy promise	✓	✓	✓
Fully-qualified engineers performing the installation	✓	✓	✓
Drain down the system	✓	✓	✓
Bleed the radiators	✓	✓	✓
Full explanation of the new boiler and how to use it	✓	✓	✓
Boiler covered by the manufacturer's warranty	10 years	8 years	6 years
Chemical flush of the system	–	–	✓
Carry out a power flush	✓	✓	–
Carry out a water test	✓	✓	✗

Feature	Premium Plus package	Premium package	Essentials package
Dispose of old parts	✓	✓	✗
Aftercare from our call centre	✓	✓	✗
Check and review the rest of the system	✓	✗	✗
System upgrade recommendations	✓	✗	✗
Full system set up to your requirements	✓	✗	✗
Onsite aftercare from a supervisor	✓	✗	✗
Routine service on the boiler's birthday	✓	✗	✗
Our price for carrying out the boiler replacement is (£x + VAT at 20%). Full T&Cs can be found on our website www.superbplumbing.xx.xx	Two easy payments of £1397	Two easy payments of £1264	£2080 – payable upfront prior to the install date

CHAPTER 21

Offer options

It's important to offer a customer extras, add-ons, optional extras and enhancements to the boiler quotation, to make sure you get the maximum willingness to pay from them. You've got your different options which you offer, but it's vital your quote speaks to the customer.

For example, if you include in your premium package a Hive or Nest heating control system and your customer categorically doesn't want one, then we immediately exclude your customer from that option meaning they will default to a cheaper package. Why would they pay for something which they don't want?

Your three package options should be suitable for all, but in order to satisfy their needs it is this section that allows them to be personalised. It's not a case of selling – it's letting people buy what they wish to. Some of these added extras will come from the conversation you had with the customer when you did the home survey for the boiler replacement.

If the customer told you they want an outside tap fitted, it would be in this section of the quote where you would offer the outside tap. Give them a price. It could just be a shopping list with a price next to each item, so it's easy for them to choose. The same applies to the Hive or Nest systems. Give them a price to purchase and install this added feature.

This is also the area of the quote where you can impress the customer with your expert knowledge of plumbing, heating and gas works with all the up-to-date products on the market so they can have a 'smart' home. Explain how a customer could save money by being more energy efficient. Educate the customer on the brand-new TRVs which have just been released onto the market and how they could benefit them.

You name it – if you think there is an additional upsell to the customer, just include it.

A brief sentence *"do you know about x? We can supply and install it for this price"* will suffice. Don't make it too long. Don't sell to the customer, let them buy if they wish to and the way to facilitate this is by letting them pick options, choices and benefits to ease their pain points.

Optional extras

This section of the quote is to offer additional products and services which don't fall within the three packages on offer. I've clarified there are three different shoppers out there: the value, standard and premium shoppers. You also meet customers who will always want a discount, a deal or something extra for free. This is the section of the quote where you would satisfy those sorts of clients. (I am one of these people; I always want a deal and will haggle to achieve this!) But, I need to make this clear – you should not offer discounts.

As an alternative, what you should offer is *behavioural rewards*, for example, *"I'll do something for you, if you do something for me"*. I wouldn't suggest calling it a behavioural reward in your quote, try something more creative like, "that little extra help", or 'your rewards".

Some examples of behavioural rewards you could include in your quotes:

• **£x discount for an honest review on online channels, including: Google/Facebook/Yell/Checkatrade/TrustATrader.** Whatever platform you use to promote your business, if you want more people to leave reviews, offer a discount for doing that. What you're doing is a win-win situation. A customer gets a lower price, but off the back end of that you also get a testimonial which, when read by potential customers, is good for the *'Know, Like and Trust'* factors. Testimonials are so powerful and as a business having a system in place to ensure that you systematically receive testimonials will do wonders.

- **£x discount for 100% of the boiler installation being paid up-front, in full, prior to the installation.** For example, if you're doing a large house renovation, with multiple bathrooms, full house re-pipes and heating installed (maybe to the tune of £20,000 or £19,897!) why don't you offer a discount if they pay you up-front? They're going to pay you anyway, that's the price agreed, so offer a discount for full payment as opposed to your standard payment terms.

- **Refer-a-friend system** – *"we can offer you a discount of £x amount for three names, numbers and email addresses of people you know who might require our services."* Explain that you can offer the discount as you can save on your marketing budget because they're giving you leads for potential custom. If you use this referral system, always ask if you can drop their name. *"Hi Mrs Drew, Mr Peacock passed on your details... ".* This reinforces the *'know, like and trust'* factors because their friend has recommended them to you and you can build up a good, quick database expansion. You could present this offer as a voucher. Include the voucher in the quote stating that you offer £x cash for referrals.

A lot of plumbing and heating businesses rely on word of mouth to grow their business. The problem with relying on word of mouth is, you base your entire business model on hope. Therefore, in my eyes, in order to have a successful business model (which relies on word of mouth or referrals), it is essential that you have a system in place to systematically deliver referrals to your business. If not, you're relying on hope, which is a dangerous business model. I'm all for referrals to build your business, but you must make sure you have referral systems in place in order to make sure the referrals systematically come to your business.

What this also generates is more people praising your company. The only thing I would be wary of is – be ready for the additional surge in telephone calls. Make sure you have the labour and capacity in place to manage any surge in demand. One of the best ways to expand a business is by doing a good job. If you're overworked or overrun, it's going to be hard to do a good job, so your reputation is on the line. Ensure your company's capacity evolves as you implement marketing techniques, so you grow in harmony.

CHAPTER 22

Warranties, guarantees and promises

In this section, you should make any details of the warranty offered by the manufacturer extremely clear to the customer. Does the boiler manufacturer offer a warranty? If they do, openly explain to the customer how long it is and how they would validate it.

For example, a lot of boiler manufacturers offering warranties stress the boiler must be serviced every year by the installing company. They also insist it needs to have a stamp showing the boiler has been serviced to validate the warranty.

Warranties and guarantees are very important. You can use them to make you stand out from the crowd. Some plumbing and heating companies offer extended manufacturer warranties if they are fully accredited by a boiler manufacturer. If this is the case for you, make this extremely clear. Highlight it to the customer. *The majority of customers buy* boilers based on the warranty.

Besides the manufacturer's warranty, the installing plumbing and heating company can also offer their own guarantees to the customer.

Show-up and turn-up guarantees

For example, I would recommend you offer a guarantee of 'show-up and turn-up'. Where you can promise the customer, you will show up on x day of the week. A lot of cowboys out there will happily receive a deposit from a customer and then not turn up on the agreed day. This causes a lot of stress for the customer who may have taken a day off work or asked Doris from next door to sit in. Offering a 'turn-up guarantee' reassures the customer.

Clean-up guarantee

A 'clean-up guarantee' is another one you could offer. Promise the customer at the end of each day you will tidy the workspace. You'll have to manage expectations if the boiler installation is going to take two or three days, let the customer know you will tidy up, but some of the materials will still be on their premises during this time.

What you're now offering are manufacturer guarantees to show-up, turn-up and clean-up. You could even offer a cash compensation in relation to the clean-up policy. If they feel you have not cleaned up properly, you could offer them £x.

I need to clarify that it is exceedingly rare for a customer to trigger these additional guarantees. They are in place to give the customer peace of mind and to make your business stand out from every Tom, Dick and Barry! Plumbing and heating is a competitive business, therefore, you must stand out to be noticed and using guarantees will assist with this.

Warranties, guarantees and promises from Superb Plumbing & Heating Ltd

Manufacturer's warranty

In partnership with Worcester Bosch, we can offer you extended cover, providing five additional years of manufacturer's warranty, making 10 years in total. We will automatically register your boiler for an extended warranty once installed and paid for. Please be aware, your boiler may need to be serviced periodically to maintain the manufacturer's warranty.

Clean-up guarantee

We will use dust sheets wherever required and promise we will fully clean up after ourselves. We guarantee this. If you feel we have not fully cleaned up after ourselves, then we will give you £50 – this is our 'Clean-Up Guarantee'. (*See* T&Cs online)

Boiler installation date guarantee

Once we have booked in your installation, we guarantee we will show up when we have told you we will. If we do not, then we will give you £50 – this is our 'Show-Up Guarantee'. (See T&Cs online)

Superb Plumbing & Heating Ltd have a fully guaranteed 'show-up and clean-up' policy.

CHAPTER 23

Frequently asked questions (FAQs)

There will be information which you want to share with the customer which does not fit into any of the other sections. Therefore, this is the section for that information.

As a starting point, I would make sure the work you're doing is clearly stated to customers. If they want anything additional or outside the scope of works, then this needs to be agreed, prior to any work being undertaken.

Managing customer expectations

It's important to manage expectations for a customer so that when you turn up on the day to replace the boiler, there are no shocks. Here are some ways you can manage expectations:

- Tell them what time you're going to arrive at their premises. As this is a quotation and has not yet been accepted, you can also inform the customer how quickly you could turn up to replace the boiler if they were to accept the quote. Stress if it's an emergency replacement and they have no hot water or heating, then you will prioritise them as a valued customer, as opposed to other customers who do have heating and hot water.

- Inform the customer that if the system needs to be drained, they will not have any hot water or heating for x amount of time.

- Explain to the customer how many people will be turning up. It may just be one heating engineer for most of the job, but an electrician will turn up on the day to wire up the boiler. You can add any further FAQs to this section of the quote.

- Use this section to inform the customer how you take your tea!

- If you require extra work to be carried out, which is not stated above then we will provide a fixed price quotation before any additional work is undertaken. Only if you sign an Extra Work Order (EWO) to confirm you are happy to pay for the extra work – on the mutually acceptable terms described in the EWO, will we carry out any work over and above anything specifically listed in this quotation. This means, you will never be billed for anything you're not expecting or have signed for.

- Any building and painting work following the installation is not included.

- This quotation does not include building works unless specified.

- To receive a bespoke building quote, please call the office.

- Whilst all due care will be taken, no responsibility can be accepted for any furnishings, fittings, fixtures or redecoration when undertaking the proposed works.

- We will endeavour to match existing exterior brickwork, cladding or rendering to the best of our efforts. However, no liability can be accepted where the precise bricks or finish materials are not available, or we have not been informed of the exact type to use.

- No responsibility can be taken for any of the existing heating or domestic plumbing systems.

- We offer a 'cooling off' period of seven working days, for cancellation of the contract incurring no penalties.

- Tea, one sugar please!

CHAPTER 24

Terms and conditions (T&Cs)

This is the legal jargon that is required within a boiler quotation. As I'm not a qualified lawyer/solicitor I can't go into too much detail in this section, but I highly recommend you get some bespoke T&Cs drawn up by a solicitor unique to your business. These terms can be re-used again and again while still valid.

To ensure the boiler quote isn't overly lengthy, you could have your T&Cs on your website, then on the boiler quotation all you have to state is "please refer to the T&Cs on our website" and include the link.

CHAPTER 25

Call to action

This section is purely to inform the customer how they accept the quote.

You will need some standard wording for this which the customer can respond to. Hopefully, you're using technology to offer an online signature link, e.g. DocuSign. You can include a DocuSign link in your quote so the customer can sign the quotation automatically.

The last thing you should do is print out a quote, post it and await the postal return of the form and a cheque. By then, an entire week has passed. This is the 21st century not the 1800s! Get with the times. Make sure it is easy to accept a quote. You will need to embrace modern technology to ensure this is quick and seamless.

Alternatively, if you're quoting for a boiler to a customer who doesn't have an email address, I suggest that you take the quote round in person and hand-deliver it. At this point, you can answer their questions and leave with a deposit.

Within the job acceptance section of the quote, you also need to inform the customer of the required deposit or first payment. Inform them they will need to sign and date the form and pay the deposit to confirm the work. As you're offering the customer options, upsells and behaviour rewards, these items need to be included in this section, with a simple tick box for people to accept ('Y' or 'N'). If you're emailing the quote over as a pdf, then I would have this section in the body of the email as well, so that responding and accepting the quote is straight forward. Do not complicate this process.

Quote acceptance form:

	Amount £ (plus VAT)	Yes please/ No thanks
Options:		
Premium Plus package	2794	Y / N
Premium package	2528	Y / N
Essentials package	2080	Y / N
Additional items:		
Outside tap	100	Y / N
Hive	150	Y / N
Nest	180	Y / N
Your rewards:		
Online review on Google and TrustATrader	-25	Y / N

I/We accept this quotation Ref No. Q12345 under the T&Cs as stated in this quote and at www.superbplumbing.xx.xx/terms&conditions.
I/We have indicated above the package, any additional items and rewards (if any) opted for.

I/We are aware of the payment terms and will abide by these.

Payment options:

- We offer the following payment options: BACS bank transfer (sort code xx-xx-xx / account xxxxxxxx), cash, cheque, credit or debit cards.

- We also offer boiler finance via third party. Please contact the office for more details.

Please refer to the DocuSign email requesting a digital signature for this quote. Once the signature and upfront payment/first payment have been received, we will contact you to arrange a mutually convenient date and time for the works to begin.

All essential steps to building the perfect boiler quotation have now been explored. The full quote example with all the different sections which need to go into a domestic boiler replacement quotation starts on page 130.

PART THREE

ADAPTING YOUR BUSINESS FOR THE FUTURE

CHAPTER 26

What gets measured gets managed

There is a saying in business *"what gets measured gets managed"* and this should be applied to your quotes. What I suggest you have is a spreadsheet – a log, of all the quotes you do. Use the spreadsheet to record the:

- Customer's name.

- Customer's address.

- Monetary amount of the quote (if you're using a three-tier pricing system, have three different columns for the three different prices).

- Surveyor's name (it is important to measure and track the performance of different surveyors – ask why one surveyor is winning more quotes than another. What are they doing different? What's working for them that the others could implement?).

Whenever you have won a quote, I suggest you use the spreadsheet to mark the quote has secured/obtained and at what level – i.e. your value, standard or premium packages. Then, constantly monitor and measure the following:

- How many quotes are you converting?

- At what level are you winning the quotes (value, standard or premium)?

- Ask a customer why you were unsuccessful.

Going back to the saying, "what gets measured gets managed" – by measuring these metrics, you can monitor how well your company is performing.

If your quote acceptance rate is 20% then something is wrong. If it is 100% and everyone is going for the premium package, there is something wrong there as well, as it shows you are too cheap.

CHAPTER 27

One-page brochure

As I mentioned earlier, scoping out the work is an essential part of the entire quoting process. To complement your quote, I suggest you produce a professionally-designed brochure for that service. Creating a brochure is much easier than you think. For example, you should have a brochure for a boiler replacement, combination-in, combination-out.

Reasons for creating a brochure

Usually, someone will arrive to undertake the home survey, ask lots of questions, take loads of measurements and leave, sending the quote via email the next day. If you have a well-designed glossy brochure (explaining your business and the services you provide for boiler replacements), you will stand out. Your competitors probably aren't doing that.

Therefore, if you produce a professional brochure and your potential customer receives three quotes, you will stand out as being a higher standard than the others. They may be more enticed to choose your quote (even if you are not the cheapest), just because you supplied a brochure and demonstrated you're a creditable company that goes that extra step. Brochures are such a powerful tool for:

- demonstrating your expertise

- promoting your quality, and

- giving your quotation a structure.

The power of context

In 1983, American Economist, Richard Thaler found customers were willing to pay different prices for the same beer depending on where it was sold. For example, if you were to go to your local pub a bottle of Peroni is more expensive than it would be in your local corner shop. It is the same product, but it is priced differently because they're in a different context.

Producing a presentable brochure puts you in a different context. The environment in which you sell your products and services is critically important. Professional material enhances the perception of quality and removes judgement of how expensive your price appears.

Promotional packaging and the four 'Ps' of marketing

Creating a well-presented brochure is known as 'packaging' or 'promotion' – one of the famous four 'P's underpinning successful marketing of any product or service. As well as 'packaging or promotion', the three others 'Ps' include: product, price and place.

Have you ever opened an Apple product? They often describe their packaging as 'exquisite'. Apple understands when you professionally package your products, it influences the customer's perception of quality. Most people will pay more for something with outstanding quality. Therefore, I recommend creating a professional-looking brochure.

Authority

Having a professional-looking brochure positions you as an expert in the plumbing and heating industry. It establishes authority. Producing a comprehensive brochure for a boiler replacement shows potential customers you're serious about boiler replacements. It is a service which you, as a business, undertake all the time and therefore, have taken the steps to produce a brochure detailing your offerings. If you hardly ever replace boilers, you would have no need to produce a boiler brochure. The brochure compliments the service you are offering.

The fact you have your services written on paper means you're not making it up as you go along. You are an expert. People are more likely to buy from an expert. Someone they deem experienced. And, people will pay more for an expert they TRUST.

Boiler replacement system

Arguably, there is an even more important reason for preparing a brochure. Your brochure becomes your system, your *aide de memoire*, so you remember what to say. Rather than relying on your memory to describe your three different packages for a boiler replacement, you have got the information in front of you to run through. It will give you a structure to guide you through the process.

I recommend you have a brochure for every major service you provide. For example, if you replace cylinders, have a brochure for this. If you replace system boilers, have a brochure for that. Even bathrooms. You name it – if it is a major service you offer, and it is something which you consistently do, I recommend you have a brochure complimenting the service.

CHAPTER 28

A bonus one-page brochure concept

I have already discussed there are three different types of shoppers. When selling to those shoppers, it's important to base your packages on the type of buyer they are, by having a few lines explaining who a particular package is designed for.

If I combine this section of the quote along with the tick-list section of the boiler replacement (where I set out what's included in the three different packages), what you've got is a small, single-page brochure. At the top, you will have the title of the service (Boiler Replacement), then three paragraphs: Essentials Package, Premium Package and Premium Plus Package. Underneath, you will have a simple tick-list of everything you'll do for a boiler replacement with your ticks and crosses. Just by combining this information, you have created a professional one-page brochure.

What I suggest you do with this one-page brochure is, when undertaking the home survey, leave it at the customer's property for them to read at their own leisure. Make sure it is fully branded and colour coordinated in line with your business-branding rules. You need to make it look good.

The one-page brochure needs to sell your company so, I recommend you get multiple copies printed up professionally on thick glossy card and make them look the part. If the one page is on a flimsy sheet of A4 paper (printed from your HP printer with refill ink), the message you get across is not one of professionalism and quality. Therefore, make it look the dog's bollocks! Also, by leaving the brochure at your potential client's property and explaining you have three different packages for the boiler replacement, when you come to give them a quote and, a choice of three different prices – it will not come as a surprise because you've left the one-page brochure there.

Basically, you can use snippets out of *The Quote Handbook* and combine them together to create more branding literature and documents for your business. I'm a big fan of repurposing information and that's exactly what we're doing here – taking two sections of a boiler quotation and putting them together to create a one-page brochure. For added *'Know, Like and Trust'* factors, include testimonials on the back page.

Below is a simple example illustrating this:

SUPERB
PLUMBING & HEATING

Keeping you warm and cosy.

Your options for a boiler replacement

Premium Plus package: This is the best option for tech-savvy property owners who enjoy the finer things in life. You want the best products, the best add-ons and the best aftercare for complete peace of mind. While onsite, we will even look at the rest of your system so you can rest assured everything will be taken care of.

Premium package: This is our most popular option and is for households that want to go beyond the essentials needed to replace the boiler. You will receive the best aftercare and we will also carry out a power flush of your entire system to ensure sludge is removed and efficiency is maximised.

Essentials package: This package is for the more budget-cautious household, happy to miss out on the added extras and instead, just want a basic boiler replacement. Rest assured, we promise to deliver the great workmanship, attention to detail and customer care we are well known for.

The table below summarises what is included in each of the packages and your options at a glance:

Feature	Premium Plus package	Premium package	Essentials package
Bespoke quotation (as stated above with further information in the appendix)	✓	✓	✓
Easy payment options	✓	✓	✓
Boiler installation date guarantee	✓	✓	✓
Clean and tidy promise	✓	✓	✓
Fully-qualified engineers performing the installation	✓	✓	✓
Drain down the system	✓	✓	✓
Bleed the radiators	✓	✓	✓
Full explanation of the new boiler and how to use it	✓	✓	✓

Feature	Premium Plus package	Premium package	Essentials package
Boiler covered by the manufacturer's warranty	10 years	8 years	6 years
Chemical flush of the system	–	–	✓
Carry out a power flush	✓	✓	–
Carry out a water test	✓	✓	✗
Dispose of old parts	✓	✓	✗
Aftercare from our call centre	✓	✓	✗
Check and review the rest of the system	✓	✗	✗
System upgrade recommendations	✓	✗	✗
Full system set up to your requirements	✓	✗	✗
Onsite aftercare from a supervisor	✓	✗	✗
Routine service on the boiler's birthday	✓	✗	✗

CHAPTER 29

Your website

Your website is of paramount importance. Most prospective customers, whether they have been referred to you or not, will look at your website to reassure themselves that you're a credible business and not some cowboy.

It is incredibly tempting to create a website yourself, but please consider this carefully. Your website is your number one marketing tool. You can use free social media accounts to drive traffic to it. If it is created by a professional, then your technical and on-page SEO (Search Engine Optimisation) will be excellent and you will be picked up by people searching for your services in that area.

An excellent website need not cost thousands to create, although many web agencies will tell you that you need to spend over £3,000 – you don't! Shop around and ask for recommendations. A highly attractive and functional website with an online booking system and links to your reviews from whatever platform you left them on, is all possible for much less.

Planning the perfect website

When you're planning your website content, always remember the points already made throughout *The Quote Handbook*:

- Tell people your solution to their pain points.

- If you can replace a broken boiler within 24 hours – make sure your website shouts about this service.

- If you have ongoing maintenance packages and will contact homeowners for their annual service automatically – tell them how they don't need to remember. You take the hassle out of them having to remember.

- Don't forget to say what areas you cover, it's pointless someone calling you from 100 miles away... unless you have teams nationwide, of course.

- And, whilst they need to know you're qualified, what professional bodies you belong to, and you're insured, don't go on about it... just make those points and move on.

Remember, every page needs to tell the customer what to do next. Do you want them to call you? Book a home survey online? Email you? Answer all those questions people ask you time and time again.

My advice when thinking about your website... look at other sites you like, which are easy to use and provide all the information a customer would need and have something similar built for yourself. A last word of warning – *never* copy text from someone else's website or blog... Google knows and will stop you showing up in searches as it's classed as 'duplicate text'.

CHAPTER 30

The future of the plumbing and heating industry

Being an expert plumbing and heating Accountant, I get a lot of exposure to the wonderful and ever-changing world of this industry. This industry fascinates me. It never stays still. It's constantly evolving. There is always something exciting around the corner, whether it be a government incentive scheme to reduce CO_2 emissions or something the manufacturers and installers are doing to drive efficiency and innovate the industry.

Just in the last couple of years, I've seen big innovations in outside taps, whereby and once an outside tap has turned off, it will automatically empty every drop of water inside preventing damage to the tap caused by freezing during the winter months.

I'm also seeing the likes of the Radbot being released onto the market. Radbot is a smart TRV which gets to know the household and its time schedule so, before you come home, your heating will automatically come on (*see* www.radbot.com).

I'm seeing merchants stocking installer's vans with their own stock, so when a breakdown engineer goes to replace a part, the part is on their van. All they have to do is use the merchant's stock, then once a week the merchant will go to the engineer's van and replenish that stock. This increasingly common practice is increasing the amount of first visit fixes for breakdowns, saving the company revisit times and making sure customer's appliances are back up and running quicker. Also, I'm noticing Uber drivers delivering breakdown parts to people's properties so the engineer doesn't have to leave the property – they can stay onsite and do other jobs.

The way the industry is moving forward is both remarkable and brilliant. This industry does not stop.

A fast-moving and innovative industry

With so many additional features, innovations and research going on across the industry, there has never been a more exciting time. However, this also means there is a constant stream of new products being launched onto the market and a pressure to inform your customers about them. If they want a home with top-of-the-range gadgets and gizmos, then there is always something around the corner which is going to be superior to the last must-have item. The work and effort which goes into this industry is unbelievable. It's important (compulsory even) that you keep up with the changes to remain relevant, maintain your success and uphold your reputation as an innovative plumbing and heating engineer or business. There's perpetual improvement across the industry, which in my eyes is good for everyone.

Providing you keep on top of the training and up-to-date with the new products coming out, I don't think you'll be short of business. Every time something new comes out, as long as you market it and want to install it in your customers' homes, you'll see surges in both custom and revenue.

There will always be premium shoppers out there who want a smart home with the most current and up-to-date technology. It's your job to make sure the customer knows about them and, likewise, that you're educated in how to install them.

PART FOUR

CASE STUDIES, USEFUL CRITIQUES, THE FINAL QUOTATION EXAMPLE AND OTHER BITS

CHAPTER 31

Case study

As an experienced Accountant in the plumbing and heating industry, I see a lot of boiler quotations. I know what makes a good quote and what makes a bad one. In early 2020, I posted on LinkedIn I would critique companies quotes for free. Quite a few people reached out to me and one person in particular (name remains confidential) sent me this quote:

QUOTATION - Thank you for your enquiry, I now have pleasure in submitting my quotation for the scope of works as asked.

Installation of new Viessman 100w 35kw system boiler, fitted with new flue and system filter - *5 years manufacturers warranty*. (Other options available)

Boiler to be installed in new utility area.

Install new gas pipe from meter to boiler.

Installation/replacement of new 250 LITRE INDIRECT UNVENTED CYLINDER - *25 years manufacturer's warranty*

Adapt system to suit new, removing all tanks in the loft space.

Installation of approx 35m2 UFH pipe. (Screening to be installed by builder, if you need a price for this I also have a builder who I use)

Underfloor heating manifold to be installed in utility area.

1st fix all pipework for radiators as discussed.

1st fix hot and cold feeds to new bathroom(does not include 1st fixing for bathroom layout).

Install new plumbing for hot water secondary return circuit.

Renew cold main and stopcock.

1st fix plumbing for kitchen and utility area.

2nd fix all radiators (radiators to be ordered separately with specific style and colour chosen by customer)

2nd fix kitchen & utility area.

Electrics - All wiring of heating controls (Nest smart learning thermostat) to be installed and commissioned by XXX Heating & Plumbing Ltd.

Once system is filled and tested. Boiler and cylinder will also be commissioned and registered by XXX Heating & Plumbing Ltd.

Boiler, Cylinder, UFH, controls, pipework & all fittings.

£5,280 inc vat

Labour £4,200 inc vat

Should anything else change or extra work needed, pricing will be discussed before any extra work will be carried out.

Any further questions please don't hesitate to email or ring.

Kind regards,

CHAPTER 32

Quote critique

I spent a short amount of time critiquing the above quote and these were my thoughts:

- The job is for a £10,000 boiler replacement. The quote does not look like a £10,000 quote! There is little detail, no images and just a few sentences of text. The desire to win the job is not apparent in the quote.

- Make it personal. Include a conversation that you had using words the customer used. *"Mr Lewis, thank you for inviting me into your home. You said your boiler breaking down couldn't have come at a worse time for you."*

- Build the pain. Has the current boiler broken down? Is it an emergency? *"We understand your boiler has broken down and as a result you have no hot water. As a family with children, we understand this needs replacing urgently."*

- If it is an emergency, let them know your availability in the quote. *"I know this is an emergency, therefore we can start the work on Thursday or Friday."*

- Explain the benefits of the features.

- The boiler comes with a five-year manufacturer's warranty. What does this mean? *"If your boiler breaks down during the first five years after installation, it will be repaired free of charge providing it has an annual service."*

- You're going to install a Nest Smart Learning Thermostat. What does this mean? *"You can control your heating from your smart phone giving you more control of your bills."*

- Don't abbreviate or use jargon. UFH? The customer doesn't know what it means. Use full words – under floor heating.

- Pricing – you have included the VAT in your price. If you exclude VAT, the price looks smaller. There are various 'price psychology' techniques you could use. Instead of £10,000 including VAT, you could write:

  1. It's two manageable payments of £3,999 + VAT.
  2. Or spread the cost with three easy payments of £2,666 + VAT.

- No call to action. What should the customer do next if they want to proceed? Should they pay at the end? Upfront? Half now, half later?

After the above was communicated, the plumbing and heating business tweaked a few sections and then sent this to the client:

> Thank you for your enquiry, I now have the pleasure in submitting my quotation for the scope of works as asked on my visit last Thursday to ADDRESS.
>
> Boiler - The boiler I have chosen for you from our discussion of your preference and good past experience, is a Viessman 100w 35kw System boiler. This will be ample to run a house of your size and will be installed and commissioned with a manufacturer's warranty of 5 years. For this warranty to be obtained the boiler must be serviced every 12 months. Yearly boiler services cost £60 + vat, and every 5th year will cost £150 + vat as will required a full strip down service. Boiler to be installed in Utility room.
>
> Hot water - As discussed we shall convert the hot water system into a pressurised unvented system. Replacing the old cylinder for a new

250l unvented indirect cylinder which will have the capacity to cope with up to 4 bathrooms. The cylinder will be installed in the same position and will come with a 25 year manufacturer's warranty in which you won't have to do anything, XXX Heating & Plumbing Ltd will simply complete the Benchmark certificate checklist that complies to building regulations and send off for you. On converting the system for you we will decommission all loft tank as will be redundant and remove from loft space.

Hot water return - adding a hot water return into a house of your size will be very economical and save lots on water usage. This will involve and additional pump and pipe run on the hot water circuit, which will make the hot water circulate to the furthest point and back to the cylinder, which when opening a tap the water shall be instantaneous.

Underfloor Heating - XXX Heating & Plumbing Ltd to supply & fit approx. 35 sq meters. This will work in conjunction with the boiler but with separate controls and room thermostat. This will be a clip rail system with lay flat pipe for the builder to screed over. The Underfloor heating manifold will be mounted in the utility room. Once commissioning XXX Heating & Plumbing Ltd will register the warranty.

General Plumbing 1st fix - On walking round the site on Thursday, there is a fair amount of work to be done to get all of downstairs 1st fixed. Boiler flow and returns to be run in to new boiler location in utility. Flow and return pipe to be run in from boiler to cylinder. Radiator flow and returns throughout with all new pipework, and chased into walls where necessary on drops. Renew cold main and extend to utility area. Run new hot & cold feeds to kitchen, bathrooms and utility.

General Plumbing 2nd fix - hang all new vertical column radiators with chrome angled radiator valves. Fill heating system and flush with a cleaner chemical, this will circulate for approximately an hour and then be drain, it will loosen and remove any debris and flux in the system. Once flushed, heating system will dosed up with inhibitor which will help prevent any corrosion and prolong the system. Connect plumbing in kitchen and utility area and machines.

Electrics/controls - XXX Heating & Plumbing Ltd will supply & fit all electrical works regarding controls downstream to the switch fused spurs. We shall install a new smart Nest learning thermostat, this will connect to your wifi and will save money and energy by learning and adapting to your schedule automatically. It also shows you how much energy is used in your home and send your cues on how to save even more. This will control the radiators heating and hot water, whilst the underfloor heating will have a Heatmiser neostat. We ask if the electrician could install us the following - 2 x switch fused spurs for 2 x 3kw back up immersion's in the airing cupboard next to cylinder. 1 x switch fused spur by the boiler. 1 x triple pole switch by Underfloor heating manifold.

Our payment terms require stage payments.

1st stage payment of 20% - deposit and agreement for works to commence - £1,580 + vat

2nd stage payment of 20% - once underfloor heating is installed - £1,580 + vat

3rd stage payment of 20% - once 1st fixing of all plumbing is complete - £1,580 + vat

4th stage payment of 20% - once boiler and cylinder are installed - £1,580 + vat

5th stage payment of 20% - once 2nd fix of all plumbing is completed. once all warranty registration certificates and gas safe certificate have been handed over.

XXX Heating and Plumbing Limited can make a start on this project as soon as next Thursday 16th April.

Should anything change or extra work required, pricing will be discussed before any extra work will be carried out.

Any further questions please do not hesitate to email or ring.

As you can see, the quote has vastly improved and this was all from just one short telephone conversation. If you would like to arrange a tailored meeting to discuss your quote template, I offer a service called 'Quote Critique Consultations'. Quote Critique Consultations are paid for in advance and are tailored to meet your individual circumstances and unique business requirements. They can be conducted either as an online Zoom call or by phone. Please note: I can only comment on domestic quotes.

At the end of your consultation, one of three things will happen:

1. you'll take away the knowledge from the consultation and implement the guidance

2. we'll agree to work together

3. you'll ask for a full refund on the basis that the consultation was of no use whatsoever. I've never had to issue a refund before, but the option is there for your peace of mind.

The fee for a Quote Critique Consultation is £179 + VAT (which is a small investment to make for a big reward!). To book your slot, please email info@togetherwecount.co.uk with 'Quote Critique' as the subject title.

CHAPTER 33

Full example quotation

Over the last few pages, you will see an example quotation I have created which demonstrates everything contained in *The Quote Handbook*. All the examples you have seen in the previous chapters have been taken from this.

SUPERB
PLUMBING & HEATING

123 New Street, Old Town, Newtoncity, NT8 4AB

www.superbplumbing.xx.xx   T: 0000 55378008   E: enquiries@superbplumbing.xx.xx

Boiler Replacement
Upgrading your Heating System

Keeping you warm and cosy.

QUOTATION NUMBER: Q12345

PREPARED FOR

Mr and Mrs Hatton
34 Water Street, Smallville, S14 0TW

DATE: XX/XX/XXXX

This quotation is valid for 14 days.

Dear Mr and Mrs Hatton

Brand-new efficient Worcester Greenstar 25i boiler quote

Thank you for inviting us into your home and allowing us to quote for a boiler replacement. Our understanding is your boiler has been condemned and so you need to replace the boiler in order to get your house back to normality as quickly as possible.

Don't worry, Superb Plumbing & Heating Ltd are here to save the day. By installing a new boiler, you will have hot water and heating again and benefit from efficiency savings. This will be achieved by carrying out the works as stated in this quotation. We are Gas Safe registered, so we are fully compliant with the up-to-date laws and regulations as dictated by our governing body, Gas Safe (www.gassaferegister.co.uk).

Further to our recent visit, we have created this bespoke quotation to replace your current boiler and other stated appliances. We have briefly explained the works below. For a more detailed explanation, please refer to the appendix.

To supply and install: a new Worcester Greenstar 25i boiler and horizontal flue along with:

• Magnetic filter
• Lime-scale reducer
• Pressure vessel
• Nonstandard pipework
• Insulation

The quoted price includes all labour for a gas engineer and electrician as well as all testing and commissioning.

Please note:

The average house price in the UK is around £318,000 (December 2020, Zoopla) and by installing a brand-new, efficient combination boiler, this can add 4% to a property's value (*source* yourepair.co.uk). Therefore, just by adding a new boiler, you could add £12,720 to the value of your property.

We've been listening to what our customers tell us and we've made some changes.

Our loyal customers tell us they do not just want us to replace a deceased boiler and then leave the property. They want more choice. They do not want a one size fits all solution. They want us to go beyond the basic replacement of a boiler and offer more of our expert knowledge and trade recommendations to improve the warmth, comfort and efficiency in their homes, resulting in happier households who also benefit from reduced energy bills all year round.

To bring your home back to normality we have come up with three packages to suit your specific needs:

Option 1 – the Premium Plus package
Option 2 – the Premium package
Option 3 – the Essentials package

A brief description of each package

The table *below* summarises what is included in each of the packages. To help you identify which option is best for you, here is a quick overview.

Premium Plus package

This is the best option for tech-savvy property owners who enjoy the finer things in life. You want the best products, the best add-ons and the best after-care for complete peace of mind. We will even look at the rest of your system while onsite so you can rest assured everything will be taken care of.

Premium package

This is our most popular option and is for households who want to go beyond the essentials needed to replace the boiler. You will receive the best aftercare and we will also carry out a power flush of your entire system to ensure sludge is removed and efficiency is maximised.

Essentials package

This package is for the more budget-cautious household, happy to miss out on the added extras and instead, just want a basic boiler replacement. Rest assured, we promise to deliver the great workmanship, attention to detail and customer care we are known for.

Your options at a glance:

What's included in the packages:	Premium Plus package	Premium package	Essentials package
Bespoke quotation (as stated above with further information in the appendix)	✓	✓	✓
Easy payment options	✓	✓	✓
Boiler installation date guarantee	✓	✓	✓
Clean and tidy promise	✓	✓	✓
Fully-qualified engineers performing the installation	✓	✓	✓
Drain down the system	✓	✓	✓
Bleed the radiators	✓	✓	✓
Full explanation of the new boiler and how to use it	✓	✓	✓
Boiler covered by the manufacturer's warranty	10 years	8 years	6 years
Chemical flush of the system	–	–	✓

What's included in the packages:	Premium Plus package	Premium package	Essentials package
Carry out a power flush	✓	✓	–
Carry out a water test	✓	✓	✗
Dispose of old parts	✓	✓	✗
Aftercare from our call centre	✓	✓	✗
Check and review the rest of the system	✓	✗	✗
System upgrade recommendations	✓	✗	✗
Full system set up to your requirements	✓	✗	✗
Onsite aftercare from a supervisor	✓	✗	✗
Routine service on the boiler's birthday	✓	✗	✗
Our price for carrying out the boiler replacement is (£x + VAT at 20%). Full terms and conditions can be found on our website www.superbplumbing.xx.xx	Two easy payments of £1397	Two easy payments of £1264	£2080 - payable upfront prior to the install date

Please Note:

For the Premium and Premium Plus packages, the first payment is due on the acceptance of the quote and the second payment is due on the installation start date.

If selecting the Essentials package, then the full balance is due on the acceptance of the quote. The appendix refers to all packages.

Warranties, guarantees and promises from Superb Plumbing & Heating Ltd

Manufacturer's warranty

In partnership with Worcester Bosch we can offer you extended cover, providing five additional years of manufacturer's warranty, making 10 years in total. We will automatically register your boiler for an extended warranty once installed and paid for. Please be aware your boiler may need periodic servicing to maintain the manufacturer's warranty.

Clean-up guarantee

We will use dust sheets wherever required and guarantee we will clean up after ourselves. If you feel we have not fully cleaned up after ourselves, then we will give you £50 – this is our 'Clean-Up Guarantee'. (*See* T&Cs online)

Boiler installation date guarantee

Once we have booked in your installation, we guarantee we will show up. If we do not, then we will give you £50 – this is our 'Show-Up Guarantee'. (*See* T&Cs online)

Superb Plumbing & Heating Ltd have a fully guaranteed 'show-up and clean-up' policy.

FAQs:

- If you require extra work to be carried out, which is not stated above then we will provide a fixed price quotation before any additional work is undertaken. Only if you sign an Extra Work Order (EWO) to confirm that you are happy to pay for the extra work – on the mutually acceptable terms described in the EWO – will we carry out any work over and above that specifically listed in this quotation. This means you will never be billed for anything you are not expecting or signed for.

- Any building and painting work following the installation is not included.

- This quotation does not include building works unless specified.

- To receive a bespoke building quote please call the office.

- Whilst all due care will be taken, no responsibility can be accepted for any furnishings, fittings, fixtures, or redecoration when undertaking the proposed works.

- We will endeavour to match existing exterior brickwork, cladding or rendering to the best of our efforts. However, no liability can be accepted where the precise bricks or finish materials are not available, or we have not been informed of the exact type to use.

- No responsibility can be taken for any of the existing heating or domestic plumbing systems.

- We offer a 'cooling off' period of seven working days, for cancellation of the contract incurring no penalties.

- Tea, one sugar please!

Quote acceptance form:

	£ Amount (+ VAT)	Yes please/ No thanks
Options:		
Premium Plus package	2794	Y / N
Premium package	2528	Y / N
Essentials package	2080	Y / N
Additional items:		
Outside tap	100	Y / N
Hive	150	Y / N
Nest	180	Y / N
Your rewards:		
Online review on Google and TrustATrader	-25	Y / N

I / We accept this quotation ref no Q12345 under the terms and conditions as stated in this quote and also at www.superbplumbing.xx.xx/terms&conditions.

I / We have clearly indicated above the package, any additional items, and rewards (if any) opted for.

I / We are aware of the payment terms and will abide by these.

Payment options:

- We offer the following payment options-. BACS bank transfer (sort code xx-xx-xx account xxxxxxxx), cash, cheque, credit, or debit card.

- We also offer boiler finance via third party. Please contact the office for more details.

Please refer to the DocuSign email requesting a digital signature of this quote. Once the signature and upfront payment/first payment is received we will contact you to arrange a mutually convenient date and time for the works to start.

Appendix:

The following information explains your bespoke boiler installation.

Existing system

Turn off services to existing system and drain. Disconnect existing boiler, hot and cold-water storage tanks, and other heating system components as necessary and remove from site. Cut back any redundant pipework as required.

The boiler

Supply and install one Worcester Greenstar 25i combination boiler. Fit into position in the kitchen.

"Heating accounts for about 55% of what a household spends in a year on energy bills, so an efficient boiler can make a big difference to your bills."

Boiler flue

Supply and install a horizontal flue.

Please note: as this appliance is high efficiency, the flue will plume due to increased water content within the waste product.

Magnetic filter

Supply one in-line magnetic filter and install into position on boiler return.

"A magnetic boiler filter is an attachment fitted directly to your central heating system. It collects various metallic particles, storing them safely so they don't form a sludge which can settle at the base of a boiler and cause major problems."

Lime-scale reducer

The boiler's cold-water supply will have a lime-scale reducer fitted in order to reduce scale build up in the heat exchanger and thus help to prolong its life.

"The heat exchanger is an integral part to a boiler and can cost over £600 to replace."

Pressure vessel

Supply and install one pressure expansion vessel complete with all associated gauges, valves, and fittings. Install into primary return pipework.

Pipework

From the position of new boiler, extend primary flow and return pipework as necessary and connect to existing as required/to hot water cylinder position.

Insulation

All hot pipework connected to the hot water cylinder for a minimum of one metre or up to where they are concealed, and any new pipework in unheated areas, to be insulated.

In addition, any new pipework in unheated areas to be insulated.

"Insulating your hot water pipes reduces heat loss and can raise water temperature 2°F-4°F hotter than uninsulated pipes can deliver, allowing you to lower your water temperature setting. You also won't have to wait as long for hot water when you turn on a tap or showerhead, which helps conserve water."

Gas supply

From the position of the existing meter, which is the correct diameter to provide sufficient volume of gas, extend gas supply as necessary, connect to boiler and test for soundness.

Electric work

Wire up boiler and all associated controls, as necessary.

Carry out electrical continuity bonding of the new heating system as required by current regulations.

Please note: this quotation does not allow for any other electrical work unless stated.

Ventilation

Supply and fit permanent grills as necessary to provide sufficient ventilation, in accordance with current regulations.

Testing and commissioning

Fill heating system and test. Refill adding anti-corrosion inhibitor.

The system will be commissioned in compliance with Building Regs xxx.

"An anti-corrosion inhibitor is a chemical compound that, when added to a heating system will decrease the corrosion rate of your pipes."

The following information explains what is included in the Essentials, Premium and Premium Plus packages:

Easy payment options

We accept cash, cheques, BACS, credit and debit card. We do not charge extra for credit cards. Payment is required when an option has been selected and any add-ons, this is to secure your selection and so we know how to proceed with your request and to book in an installation date.

We also offer finance, via a third party.

Boiler installation date guarantee

Once we have booked in your installation, we guarantee that we will show up. If we don't, then we will give you £50 – this is our 'Show-Up Guarantee'. (*See* T&Cs online)

Clean-up guarantee

We will use dust sheets wherever required and promise that we will fully clean up after ourselves. We guarantee that we will clean up. If you feel we haven't fully cleaned up after ourselves, then we will give you £50 – this is our 'Clean-Up Guarantee'. (*See* T&Cs online)

Fully-qualified engineers performing the installation

All our engineers are fully-qualified tradespeople who have dedicated years of their lives to be qualified in gas, oil, LPG, electrics and renewables technologies.

Drain down the system

In order to replace the boiler, the water in the system often needs to be drained.

Bleed the radiators

As part of the boiler replacement and to ensure that the heating system is fully tested, we will bleed the radiators; this is the reverse effect of the drain down, mentioned above. This means all excess air in the system will be removed. This will be performed after the boiler has been installed.

Full explanation of the new boiler and how to use it

We will show you what we have replaced and explain the new controls, providing a full explanation of how to use your new appliances.

Chemical flush of the system

Inhibitor removes sludge, scale and debris from the existing central heating system to restore heating efficiency and eliminate boiler noise. The inhibitor we use is a non-hazardous product which is compatible with all metals commonly used in heating systems.

The following information explains what is included in the Premium and Premium Plus packages:

Carry out a power flush

A power flush is a cleansing process which removes sludge build up inside your central heating system over time. A power flush is an ideal solution to clean and maintain your central heating system to improve the amount of heat permitted from your radiators.

Carry out a water test

We will test the water in your system for contaminants, reporting back the findings and a resolution if required.

Dispose of old parts

We will take away all old parts and dispose of them in an environmentally-friendly manner. Any packaging will be recycled.

Aftercare from our call centre

In the weeks after the boiler installation, our knowledgeable call centre team will ring you to ensure that everything is running as it should be. Any questions will be answered and addressed.

The following information explains what is included in the Premium Plus package only:

Check and review the rest of the system

Our trained engineers will review the rest of your heating and hot water system to ensure there are no leaks, faults, damage or problems. We will look at your heating system through thermal heat-seeking goggles to identify anomalies. This is an extremely valuable service. Customers can benefit from having a thermal inspection done. Heat-seeking goggles detect temperature by recognising and capturing different levels of infrared light (invisible to the naked eye) which are felt as heat when the intensity is high enough. This valuable service allows engineers to detect thermal defects, heat losses and air leakages and then determine whether better insulation is needed. The technique can also be used to ensure insulation has been installed properly and to check the effectiveness of your overall home insulation.

System upgrade recommendations

While reviewing your system our engineers will recommend:

- New technologies to get the best out of your system.
- Any energy-saving tips and tricks, saving you money.
- Discuss your current heating and hot water requirements.

Full system set up to your requirements

The buttons on the boiler and thermostats can be confusing. Our engineer will fully customise the heating system to your personal preference. For example, the radiators can be set to automatically come on at 7am and turn off at 10am. The choice is yours.

Onsite aftercare from a supervisor

In the weeks following the boiler installation, a supervisor will revisit your property to ensure that everything is running as it should be. Any questions can be answered and addressed.

Routine service on the boiler's birthday

We will attend your property the following year to service the boiler. This is a requirement to validate the manufacturer's warranty. (*See* T&Cs online)

CHAPTER 34

What next?

Thank you for taking the time to read *The Quote Handbook*. I hope you have gained some valuable insight which you can implement in your business to improve your quotes and ensure they cover all the vital areas. If you connect with me on social media (LinkedIn and Facebook) I will provide you with the following:

LinkedIn

I will send you an Excel pricing template which will enable you to price up a boiler replacement, including the three options (value, standard and premium). Be sure to mention *The Quote Handbook* in your message so I know you have read the book.

Scan this QR code to follow me on LinkedIn:

www.linkedin.com/in/aaron-mcleish-specialist-accountant-3a0ab529

Facebook

I will provide a quote template for the boiler replacement complete with all the above-mentioned sections of a boiler quotation. This will save you having to re-type the information shared in *The Quote Handbook*!

Let's keep the conversation going and connect with others who have read *The Quote Handbook*. There is a dedicated Facebook group for readers to connect and discuss the content of the book, while offering support and discussions as you implement changes to your business.

Scan this QR code to join the dedicated Facebook group for fellow readers of *The Quote Handbook*:

**www.facebook.com/groups/
TheQuoteHandbook**

Take a look at my business page to find out how I can help you tap into your full business potential.

www.facebook.com/togetherwecount

Website

Scan this QR code to visit the *Together We Count* website:

www.togetherwecount.co.uk

Blog

Subscribe to my blog for the most up-to-date advice and information affecting plumbing and heating businesses today.

Scan this QR code to visit my blog:

www.togetherwecount.co.uk/blog

Amazon

Please review *The Quote Handbook* on Amazon and I will send you a sales conversion analytic spreadsheet (*see* Chapter 26 What gets measured gets managed).

Just email info@togetherwecount.co.uk with a link to your Amazon review and we will reply with an excel analytic spreadsheet attachment.

How to use a QR code:

1. Open the QR reader on your smartphone. (If you don't have one, you can easily download one for free in the App Store or Play Store).

2. Hold your device over the QR code so that it is visible on your screen.

3. If you have done this correctly, the smartphone will automatically scan the QR code. You may need to press a button, much like taking a photograph. The smartphone will navigate you to the intended destination.

Together We Count are accountants who specialise in the plumbing and heating industry. *Together We Count* can help you and your business with:

Compliance

- Tax returns
- VAT returns
- Construction Industry Scheme (CIS) returns
- Company secretarial
- Year-end accounts

Running your business

- Management accounts
- Payroll
- Auto-enrolment
- Bookkeeping
- Budgets
- Credit control
- Cost control
- Finance Director
- Company formations
- Benchmarks

Growing your business

- Business plans
- Cash-flow forecasts
- Company valuations
- Profitability analysis
- Business advisory
- Business coaching
- Price consulting

Saving money

- Tax planning
- Business cost reduction

Together We Count services

I practice what I preach, therefore, here are the benefits of the services TWC provide:

Management accounts – when running a plumbing and heating business, it's vital you have up-to-date management accounts. Management accounts reveal how your business is performing for a specific period, meaning you are informed to make sound business decisions.

Bookkeeping – is a vital part of any plumbing and heating business. Basically, it accounts for what comes in and what goes out. (Ideally more should come in!) Are you keeping a track of this?

Credit control – it's especially important every plumbing and heating business keeps close tabs on customers who owe them money. Do you have a sound credit control system in place? If not, you could be owed thousands. Money should be in your bank account not your customer's!

Company formations – are you currently trading as a sole trader or partnership? Trading as a limited company offers you protection, the ability to expand, be more prestigious, and affords you the opportunity to save more in tax.

Benchmark – being an expert plumbing and heating Accountant, I prepare and produce a lot of accounts for businesses in this sector. Therefore, I can benchmark your business against other plumbing and heating businesses and let you know how you're performing against your peers.

Tax returns – are your company tax returns as tax efficient as possible? Are you buying plant and machinery at the right time to maximise tax benefits? Are you paying as little corporation tax as possible?

VAT returns – as an experienced plumbing and heating Accountant, I know which circumstances you can charge 5% VAT. Are you charging your customers too much in VAT?

CIS returns – does your plumbing and heating business hire sub-contractors? If so, you are legally obliged to deduct either 0%, 20%, or 30% tax off your sub-contractors and pay it to HMRC periodically. Are you being compliant?

Year-end accounts – do you want a specialist plumbing and heating Accountant to prepare your year-end financial accounts, so you comply with HMRC and Companies House?

Payroll – if you employ staff, you need to operate a payroll scheme. Likewise, if you are a Director you could be paid a tax-efficient salary which is processed via your payroll scheme.

Cost control – is your plumbing and heating business as lean as possible regarding expenses, costs and discounts/rebates from suppliers and merchants? Are you receiving a top rebate for your boiler installations?

Together We Count are expert plumbing and heating Accountants. We also offer business advice, where we can sit down, discuss your goals, establish where you want to be in work/life and devise a strategy to get you there. It's a huge topic and if you want to know more, get in touch today and see how TWC can help your business thrive.

Boost your business

I often find when gas engineers start up in business, they have massive drive and ambition. Many plumbing and heating businesses churn out jobs and work to please their customers, with no realistic pricing policy or business systems. This often leads to feelings of regret for going into business. They dream of turning over £1million plus per annum, of owning the best-sign written vans, having office staff and a team of loyal, trustworthy engineers working for them – and of being the boss! They want the financial freedom, wish to retire young and leave a legacy behind which will make their family proud.

Most plumbing and heating engineers are excellent on the tools, but with the running of the business, they fall short. Regarding the quoting and pricing side of the business, again and again I see plumbing and heating businesses crash and burn on price just to win a job and fill up their diaries for the next week or two. This can be counterproductive because people end up doing jobs with little or no margin just to keep the wages paid and the lights on. People aren't pricing for maximum profit, instead they are assuming customers want the cheapest price. It is disheartening to see within their financial accounts, how they have not considered the time, effort and investment put into their business so that they are truly rewarded for their hard work.

Together We Count are here to help your business reach its peak potential. By addressing the following questions and issues, TWC will optimise your company's success and maximise your profits:

- Is your plumbing and heating business quoting to obtain maximum profit?

- Are you getting the maximum willingness to pay from your customers?

- Are you using price psychology to make your prices seem smaller?

- Are you using payment terms to make your pricing seem smaller?

- Do you need help in implementing the teachings within this book?

Systemise your business for success

- Is your plumbing and heating business systemised?

- Do you have documented systems and processes for everything you do within your business?

- Do you have a set way of doing things?

- Having a systemised business brings efficiencies, consistency and less frustration and hassle for business owners.

- Do you want to implement more systems in your business so everyone is singing off the same hymn sheet?

Beat break-even and maximise your profits

- Do you know the break-even point of your business?

- It's important to know how to ensure your costs are covered.

- It's also important to know you are charging for your services correctly to ensure you are profitable. You might have a full diary, but unless your pricing is on point you could lose money.

Converting your quotes into sales

I wrote *The Quote Handbook* because a lot of companies and individuals don't know how to quote effectively – in a way that works favourably on your conversion rate (by this I mean converting your quotes to sales). This means there is money left on the table. I have repeated this saying more than once, but it is true of so many businesses.

Along with all the traditional services you would expect from an Accountant, TWC like to take things further. We like to take the information obtained from your bookkeeping, your year-end accounts, along with other data and information gathered along the way, to paint a picture of your business. The downside to bookkeeping and year-end accounts is it is historical data. It looks at your business after it has happened. You can't change the past, but by using the information within the accounts, we can work closely with our clients to help you predict and prepare for the future.

Taking your business from 'A' to 'B'

Together We Count interpret the accounts and analyse the information to assist with your business development. *Together We Count* sees business development as getting your business from 'A' to 'B'.

'A' is where you are right now and 'B' is where you want to be. 'B' could be an increase in sales, increase in profit and, as a business owner, you may want to work less hours, take more holidays, win awards as well as be recognised as the best plumbing and heating business in your area.

Whatever your 'B' is, *Together We Count* will work with you to devise a business plan to assist your journey. A business development plan with *Together We Count* looks at the nine drivers of profit:

1. Generating more sales leads.
2. Converting sales leads into customers.
3. Getting customers to spend more.
4. Getting customers to spend more often.
5. Ensuring customers remain customers for longer.
6. Pricing for maximum profit.
7. Variable costs.
8. Fixed costs.
9. Systemise everything.

Focusing on these nine areas will ultimately lead to a more successful business. For some, they focus on one area per month, for others, they're already excelling in one area but have completely overlooked another.

Together We Count's tailored approach

Togther We Count like to get to know you and your business. Rather than an 'one size fits all' solution, TWC put together a tailored plan, bespoke to you and your business. Your business is as unique as you, so having a unique Accountant is a logical choice.

Togther We Count offer expert advisory knowledge specific to the industry to ensure your business is as good as it can be. If you would like to know more about how TWC can help you, please get in touch today at: info@togetherwecount.co.uk or visit: www.togetherwecount.co.uk.

"Our mission is to help you achieve your goals and succeed."

Aaron McLeish

Managing Director at *Together We Count*
and Author of *The Quote Handbook*

CHAPTER 35

Testimonials for *Together We Count*

Earlier in *The Quote Handbook,* I mentioned the importance of receiving testimonials from your customers (*see* Chapter 11). Testimonials show potential customers you have the *Know, Like and Trust* factor. They are also proof that customers have confidence in your business and trust in the professional services you offer.

TWC cover a diverse range of projects with a professional approach and high-quality services that never change. However, rather than me trying to convince you, TWC's great reputation and recommendations come directly from our customers and what they say about us.

The following testimonials (which you will find on Google) are from customers and businesses who put their trust in TWC:

"Great service and value for money. I was kept updated regularly throughout the process and TWC are very helpful in explaining the (sometimes confusing) accounting jargon. Highly recommend and I will be using TWC going forward."

Aeion, plumbing and heating business

"Aaron McLeish has been a fountain of knowledge when it comes to helping my business optimise cash-flow and plan for sustainable, predictable growth. He has been instrumental in helping Lead Hero setup our accounting system and pricing us with the trusted advice we need as take our business from strength to strength. Aaron is not only our adviser and expert accountant, but I'm happy to call him a friend. I know many people who have already benefited from putting into action the knowledge contained in this book, and I sincerely hope you will listen, digest and most of all, take action to acerbate your sales and design the 'perfect quote'."

Francis, Founder of Lead Hero, (www.leadhero.ai) helping established trades and businesses to accelerate sales, get control and free up more time to grow a business that runs itself.

"As a self employed electrician I don't have time for a lot of things, especially getting my paperwork in order, but Aaron of the Sheffield branch of Together We Count sorted me out. I have had various firms to do my accounts who have not given me the kick I needed, but I cannot praise Aaron enough for pushing me to get things together before my deadline passed so I did not get another fine as I have done in the past! The hard work was taken away from me, and all I basically had to do was read and sign. I would 100% recommend Together We Count as they have been more helpful than I deserve with my "I will do it tomorrow" attitude, and they go above and beyond to do everything correctly and on time! Nothing was too much trouble whenever I asked."

Liam, electrician

"Finding an accountant can be a difficult and stressful process, Together We Count took care of everything and were able to give excellent advice with starting up a new limited company. All of my questions were answered, and Aaron was always happy to quickly respond to all of my concerns. Aaron is an expert in his field of accounting especially so with plumbing and heating companies.

Aaron has been able to help me see the light after being let down by my previous accountant. He has helped with setting up software to help in the general running of the business and even given valuable knowledge with winning more work. I have now managed to take on my first new member of staff and Together We Count have taken care of all the paperwork involved to get payroll set up. I would highly recommend anyone who is looking for a new accountant to get in touch with Together We Count even if they are not local to you!"

Lewis, plumbing and heating business

CHAPTER 36

List of abbreviations and acronyms

CEO	Chief Executive Officer
CIS	Construction Industry Scheme
CRM	Customer Relationship Management
EWO	Extra Work Order
FCA	Financial Conduct Authority
FAQs	Frequently Asked Questions
FOMO	Fear of Missing Out
LPG	Liquefied Petroleum Gas
PDQ	Process Data Quickly
T&Cs	Terms and Conditions
TWC	Together We Count
SEO	Search Engine Optimisation
TRVs	Thermostatic Radiator Valves
UFH	Under Floor Heating
VAT	Value Added Tax

Printed in Great Britain
by Amazon